#1 Self Taught Arabic Book

Nisreen Beshqoy

Additional copies of this book can be purchased via the internet at:
www.number1selftaughtarabicbook.com

For any questions you may have, the author can be reached via e-mail
nisreenbeshqoy@hotmail.com

Library of Congress Control Number: 2004095420

ISBN: 0-9759181-0-9

Printed in the United States by
Morris Publishing
3212 East Highway 30
Kearney, NE 68847
1-800-650-7888

About the Author

Nisreen Beshqoy was born and raised in Jordan.

She graduated from high school with high honors in the Arabic language exit exam. She was accepted at the University of Jordan / School of Law, where she obtained her law degree.

Shortly after her graduation in 1990, she was married to Yousef and immigrated to Southern California -The United States of America. Now, a proud mother being blessed with three beautiful daughters Natalia, Noor, and Safa.

Dedication

I dedicate this book to my loving husband Yousef and my precious daughters Natalia, Noor, and Safa.

Introduction

The Arabic language is gaining significant attention and interest in the western world, especially within the last few years. More people are becoming more interested in learning the language for varied reasons.

Among some of these reasons are: for tourism / travel , economic/ business dealings, employment opportunities, understanding the Arabic culture, and finally understanding Islam, which is the leading religion in the Arabic countries and it is expanding into the western world. Keeping in mind that there are about 300 million Arabs and 21 Arab countries in this world.

I was compelled to write this book after discovering that the existing Arabic teaching books were too complicated to learn from .This book is an original of it's kind. It teaches Arabic in a very simplified way especially for the independent learner. It is very easy to follow along . It is also an ideal book that could be used as a text for colleges and universities.

It is intended to teach the beginners of the non-Arabic speaking person and to those Arabs raised in the western countries.

I tried to present all of the essential information needed to develop the skills of Arabic reading, mastering a step by step method including many examples to help comprehend the rules.

This book covers the basic principles of grammar and it was intentionally kept brief in order to simplify learning the Arabic language in a unique method.

The book includes over 1300 vocabulary words with its pronunciation and definitions. In addition, the appendix at the end of the book includes common words and phrases to make learning Arabic more simplified and enjoyable.

I am confident that you will love this book and will recommend it to your family and friends. Best of wishes to you.

Nisreen Beshqoy

Table of Contents

Introduction

Lesson One
The Arabic Alphabet
الحـروف العربيـــة

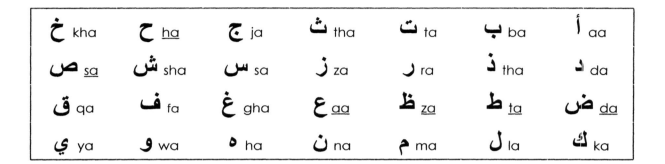

خ kha	ح ha	ج ja	ث tha	ت ta	ب ba	أ aa
ص sa	ش sha	س sa	ز za	ر ra	ذ tha	د da
ق qa	ف fa	غ gha	ع aa	ظ za	ط ta	ض da
ي ya	و wa	ه ha	ن na	م ma	ل la	ك ka

The Arabic alphabet consists of twenty-eight letters and they are all consonants. They cannot achieve a full sound without vowels, which are represented by signs written above or below the consonant. These signs are called, in Arabic: (harakat).

The Arabic script is cursive and is read from right to left. All of the letters are joined together to form words.

However, there are six letters that can join their proceeding letters in a word, but they can not join their successors.

These letters are:

١ aa	د da	ذ tha	ر ra	ز za	و wa

Some letters do not have the English analogue, however, some of these letters exist in other languages.

These letters are:

| ح <u>h</u>a | ص <u>s</u>a | ض <u>d</u>a |
| ط <u>t</u>a | ظ <u>z</u>a | ع <u>a</u>a |

In order to make it easy and simple, I used the closest familiar English letters with <u>lines</u> under the letters to express an <u>emphasis</u> and to pronounce the letter <u>very deep down the throat</u>.

The Name Of The Alphabet

Name Of The Alphabet	Pronunciation	Arabic Alphabet
alif	aa	أ
ba	ba	ب
ta	ta	ت
tha	tha	ث
jeem	ja	ج
ḥa	ḥa	ح
kha	kha	خ
dal	da	د
thal	tha	ذ
ra	ra	ر
zain	za	ز
seen	sa	س
sheen	sha	ش
ṣad	ṣa	ص
ḍad	ḍa	ض
ṭa	ṭa	ط
ẓa	ẓa	ظ
ᶜin	ᶜa	ع
ghain	gha	غ
fa	fa	ف
qaf	qa	ق
kaf	ka	ك
lam	la	ل
meem	ma	م
noon	na	ن
ha	ha	ه
waw	wa	و
ya	ya	ي

Lesson Two
Connecting Letters
وصـل الحـروف

When the letters are combined to form words, they are slightly different in appearance than when they are written independently .

The letters appear different when they are used in the beginning of the word versus in the middle and at the end of the word . Example, the letter ka (كـ)

in the beginning :	kataba (wrote)	كَتَّـــبَ
in the middle :	shakara (thanked)	شَـــكَرَ
at the end :	falak (space)	فَلَـــك

In the next page, it illustrates the shapes of all the letters when they appear at the beginning, middle and at the end of a word .

Standing alone	End	Middle	Begining
أ aa	أمريكــا America	مـاء water	أمل hope
ب ba	كلـب dog	سـباق race	بـاب door
ت ta	تـوت berries	كتـاب book	تيــن figs
ث tha	أثـاث furniture	مثـل example	ثــلاث three
ج ja	تـاج crown	سـنجاب squirrel	جَميـل beautiful
ح ḥa	نـوح Noah	سَحاب cloud	حَليـب milk
خ kha	خوخ plums	نخلـة palm tree	خـبز bread
د da	حديـد iron	مَدخل entrance	دولاب wheel
ذ tha	لذيـذ delicious	بـذر seeds	ذبابــة fly
ر ra	حِمار donkey	تـراب dirt	رَبيــع spring
ز za	موز banana	مَزاد auction	زَئبــق lily
س sa	شمـس sun	مسلم Muslim	سـمك fish
ش sha	فـراش mattress	مشمش apricot	شَمسـيه umbrella
ص ṣa	لـص robber	مصر Egypt	صـيد hunting
ض ḍa	مَـرَض illness	مُضر harmful	ضِرس molar/tooth
ط ṭa	بـط ducks	مَطار airport	طـير bird
ظ ẓa	لفـظ pronunciation	مُظلم dim	ظـهر noon
ع aa	زَرع plants	مَعـنى meaning	علم knowledge
غ gha	صـبغ dye	مُغامرة challenge	غـراب crow
ف fa	مَلـف file	مفتـاح key	فلـم film
ق qa	رَفيـق companion	دَقيـق flour	قَلــم pencil/pen
ك ka	مَـلاك angel	مكتـوب letter	كِـنز treasure
ل la	دَليـل guide	حَليـب milk	لـوز almonds
م ma	سـم poison	سمسـم sesame	ملـح salt
ن na	فـن art	كنـاري canary	نـور light
ه ha	نحلـه bee	نهـر river	هرة cat
و wa	جرو puppy	قـوي strength	ولد boy
ي ya	حي alive	سـيل torrential stream	يـرفع to lift

Lesson Three
The Prolongation Letters
أحرف المـد

The alif (ا), the waw (و), and the ya (ي) are part of the 28 Arabic consonants . They are described as long vowel signs . These three letters are used as lengtheners when they come after other consonants . The alif (ا) has the sound of (aa) . The (و) has the sound of (oo) . The (ي) has the sound of (ee) .

Examples when prolongation letters (ي , و , ا) come after the alphabet 'ba' (ب) and 'ta' (ت) :

English Translation	Pronunciation	Connected Letters	Un-Connected Letters
door	baab	بـاب	ب ا ب
owl	boom	بـوم	ب و م
well	beer	بـيـر	ب ي ر
crown	taaj	تـاج	ت ا ج
raspberry	toot	تـوت	ت و ت
fig	teen	تيـن	ت ي ن

"Ba" (ب) as in bed and big .
"Ta" (ت) as in tank and tape .

'Ta' is the most common feminine sign when it comes at the end of a word and it has also this shape (ة) as in the word عالِمـة (alimah) . It is called : closed ta .

Examples when prolongation letters (ي , و , ا) come after the alphabet 'tha' (ث) and 'ja' (ج) :

English translation	Pronunciation	Connected Letters	Un-Connected Letters
to get excited	thaar	ثار	ث ا ر
garlic	thoom	ثوم	ث و م
play a part	tamtheel	تمثيــل	ت م ث ي ل
chicken	jaaj	جاج	ج ا ج
generosity	jood	جود	ج و د
generation	jeel	جيــل	ج ي ل

"Tha" (ث) as in think and thought .
"Ja" (ج) as in job and Jordan .

Examples when prolongation letters (ي , و , ا) come after the alphabet 'ha' (ح) and 'kha' (خ) :

English translation	Pronunciation	Connected Letters	Un-Connected Letters
hot	<u>h</u>aar	حار	ح ا ر
whale	<u>h</u>oot	حوت	ح و ت
when	<u>h</u>een	حيـن	ح ي ن
to fear	khaaf	خاف	خ ا ف
plum	khowkh	خوخ	خ و خ
horses	khail	خيـل	خ ي ل

Some letters like the 'ha' (ح) and the 'kha' (خ) do not exist in the English Language. Their Pronunciation is therefore more difficult than the other letters. When pronouncing these letters, the sound originates from the depth of the throat, almost as if the person is clearing the throat.

Examples when prolongation letters (ي , و , ا) come after the alphabet 'da' (د) and 'tha' (ذ):

English translation	pronunciation	connected letters	Un-Connected Letters
house	daar	دار	د ا ر
below	doon	دون	د و ن
religion	deen	دين	د ي ن
melt	thaab	ذاب	ذ ا ب
taste	thooqu	ذوق	ذ و ق
tail	thail	ذيل	ذ ي ل

"Da" (د) as in doom and door. It is part of the stubborn letters that join it's preceding letters, but never join it's successors.
"Tha" (ذ) as in that and the. It is also part of the stubborn letters. We must distinguish it from the letter "tha" (ث) as in think and through .

Examples when prolongation letters (ي , و , ا) come after the alphabet 'ra' (ر) and 'za' (ز) :

English translation	pronunciation	connected letters	Un-Connected Letters
leave	raa<u>h</u>	راح	ر ا ح
soul	roo<u>h</u>	روح	ر و ح
feather	reesh	ريش	ر ي ش
to increase	zaad	زاد	ز ا د
untruth	zoor	زور	ز و ر
oil	zait	زيت	ز ي ت

"Ra" (ر) as in room and ring .
"za" (ز)as in zebra and zoo .   .
Both of these letters are part of the six stubborn letters .

Examples when prolongation letters (ي , و , ا) come after the alphabet 'sa' (س) and 'sha' (ش) :

English Translation	Pronunciation	Connected Letters	Un-Connected Letters
toxic	saam	سـام	س ا م
market	sooq	سـوق	س و ق
sword	saif	سـيف	س ي ف
to spread	sha__a__	شـاع	ش ا ع
thorn	shoak	شـوك	ش و ك
gray hair	shaib	شـيب	ش ي ب

"Sa" (س) as in sip and soon .
"Sha" (ش) as in shall and short .

Examples when prolongation letters (ي , و , ا) come after the alphabet '_sa_' (ص) and '_da_' (ض) :

English Translation	Pronunciation	Connected Letters	Un-Connected Letters
to fast	_s_aam	صـام	ص ا م
voice	_s_oat	صـوت	ص و ت
summer	_s_aif	صـيف	ص ي ف
harmful	_d_aar	ضـار	ض ا ر
light	_d_oo	ضـوء	ض و ء
difficulty	_d_eequ	ضـيق	ض ي ق

"_Sa_" (ص) as in sun and subway, with more emphasis, and stress of the tongue on the "s" .

"_Da_" (ض) as in sword and double, with more emphasis and stress of the tongue on the "d" .

9

Examples when prolongation letters (ي , و , ا) come after the alphabet 'ta' (ط) and 'za' (ظ) :

English Translation	pronunciation	Connected Letters	Un-Connected Letters
to fly	taar	طار	ط ا ر
length	tool	طول	ط و ل
mud	teen	طيـن	ط ي ن
unfair	zalem	ظـالِم	ظ ا لِ م
visible	manzoor	منظـور	م ن ظ و ر
cleaning	tanzeef	تنظيــف	ت ن ظ ي ف

"Ta" (ط) as in but and cut ,with more emphasis and stress of the tongue on the "t" .

"Za" (ظ) as in thus and those , with more emphasis and stress of the tongue on the "th" .

Examples when prolongation letters (ي , و , ا) come after the alphabet 'aa' (ع) and 'gha' (غ) :

English translation	pronunciation	Connected Letters	Un-Connected Letters
to return	aad	عاد	ع ا د
stick	ood	عود	ع و د
holiday	eid	عيـد	ع ي د
absent	ghaab	غاب	غ ا ب
aid, help	ghaoth	غوث	غ و ث
anger	gheaz	غيـظ	غ ي ظ

"Aa" (ع) is one of the difficult letters to pronounce . The sound stems from the depth of the throat as if one is about to clear ones throat . Depending on the prolongation letter that comes after the letter (ع) , I used the (aa) , (oo) ,and (ee) in order to assist the arabic learner how to pronounce the word .

"Gh" (غ) is another difficult letters to pronounce . The sound also stems from the depth of the throat as if one is to garggle .

Examples when prolongation letters (ي , و , ا) come after the alphabet 'fa' (ف) and 'qa' (ق) .

English Translation	Pronunciation	Connected Letters	Un-Connected Letters
to win	faaz	فــاز	ف ا ز
above	foaqu	فـوق	ف و ق
elephant	feel	فيــل	ف ي ل
to measure	qaas	قـاس	ق ا س
food	qoot	قـوت	ق و ت
chain	qaid	قيــد	ق ي د

"Fa" (ف) as in fork and forgive.
"Qa" (ق) the nearest sound is the 'c' as in calm and column with the emphasis from the throat on the "c" .

Examples when prolongation letters (ي , و , ا) come after the alphabet 'ka' (ك) and 'la' (ل):

English Translation	Pronunciation	Connected Letters	Un-Connected Letters
to be	kaan	كـان	ك ا ن
cottage	kookh	كوخ	ك و خ
bag	kees	كيــس	ك ي س
to blame	laam.	لام	ل ا م
board	loa<u>h</u>	لـوح	ل و ح
mellow	leen	ليــن	ل ي ن

"La" (ل) as in lemon and lesson. When the "alif" (ا) follows "l" (ل) they are written as "la" (لا) it means no in English.

"ka" (ك) as in kebab and key.
When the ka (ك) comes at the beginning or in the middle of the word it looks like this : بكــى (cried) .

Examples when prolongation letters (ي , و , ا) come after the alphabet 'ma' (م) and 'na' (ن) :

English Translation	Pronunciation	Connected Letters	Un-Connected Letters
money	maal	مال	م ا ل
waves	moaj	موج	م و ج
mile	meel	ميل	م ي ل
fire	naar	نار	ن ا ر
gleam /light	noor	نور	ن و ر
Nile river	neel	نيل	ن ي ل

"Na" (ن) as in noise and nest.
"Ma" (م) as in money and miss.

Examples when prolongation letters (ي , و , ا) come after the alphabet 'ha' (ه) , 'wa' (و) and 'ya' (ي).

English Translation	Pronunciation	Connected Letters	Un-Connected Letters
important	haam	هام	ه ا م
cardamom	hail	هيل	ه ي ل
valley	wadi	وادِ	و ا دِ
grief, doom	wail	ويل	و ي ل
o, oh	yaa	يا	ي ا
day	youm	يوم	ي و م

"Ha" (ه) as in house and home.
"Wa"(و) as in was and when. It is also one of the stubborn letters.
"Ya" (ي) as in yes and young.

Lesson Four
The Letter Alif
الحـرف ألـفْ

    The first letter of the Arabic alphabet alif (ا), is considered a long vowel and it is pronounced as "aa" . However, when it carries the symbol hamzeh (ء) on top of the letter (أ), it is considered a consonant and it is pronounced as short vowel "a" .

    The alif (ا) is also pronounced as a short vowel "a" if it comes at the beginning of the speech even without a hamzeh . When the alif (ا) follows l (ل) it forms a new letter la (لا) which means no in English .

    In some words the alif (ا) is not written in its normal shape . It uses the letter ya (ى) without the dots , and a hamzeh (ء) on top of the ya (ئ) . This alif becomes known as the shortened alif (الألــف المَقصـــورة) . Therefore , this shortened alif is another version of this letter .

    There is another name for the alif called " the stretched alif" (ألألــف المَمـدودة) , It comes with the "maddeh" sign (آ) above it when the alif is not vowed and hamzeh comes immediately after it. The pronunciation of this stretched alif is lengthened in those words that contain them . Examples :
dessert (ṣaḥraa-صــحرآء) and red (ḥamraa-حمرآء).

Lesson Five
Rules of Hamzeh
قواعِـد الهمزه

The hamzeh (ء) has the sound of the sudden stop during pronunciation .
The hamzeh (ء) is placed above the letters (ئ, ؤ, أ)

These three letters serve as a seat or carrier for the hamzeh (ء).
The hamzeh (ء) may occur at the beginning, in the middle, or at the end of the word.

Sometimes the alif in the beginning of the speech is used without a hamzeh and it is still pronounced as if it has a hamzeh . In addition , when you have a vowel on top of the alif , a hamzeh is always written on the top of the alif at the beginning of the word no matter what its vowels may be.

Examples :
father (abb-أب), mother (umm - أُم) , and human (insan-إنسـان) .

When the hamzeh is in the middle of the word, it comes on its seats:
-On the alif (أ), if the preceding vowel is "fet-ha"
-On the waw (ؤ), if the preceding vowel is "dammeh"
-On the ya (ئ), if the preceding vowel is "kasrah", but in this case the ya loses its two dots.

Examples :
(sa-al -سَـال)   : to ask
(bo-os-بُـؤس)   : miserable
(na-im - نـائم) : sleep

On the other hand, the middle hamzeh comes without a seat when it comes with a fet-hah vowel after a long vowel (ي , و , ا). examples :

(tasa-al - تَسـاءَل) : wonder .
(moro-ah - مُروءة) : chivalry/generosity .

When the hamzeh comes at the end of a word, it is written above one of its seats letters depending on the short vowels that comes before the hamzeh.

examples :

(qara-a - قَــرأ) : to read
(malo-a - مَلــوَ) : fill in
(nashi -ءيـــناشِ): youth

We place the hamzeh on the line without a carrier if the preceding vowel is sukoon (ْ) as it shows in the first two examples or a long vowel (ي , و , ا) as it shown on the last three examples .

(jozo-ءزْـجُ) : portion
(ebi - ءبْـعِ) : burden
(binaa- ءاــنـبِ) : building
(wo-doo - ءوــضـوُ) : ablution
(ba-ree- ءيرـبَ) : innocent

Lesson Six
The Short Vowel Signs
الحركـــات القصـــــيرة

These short vowels are important in order to pronounce the word properly. It's especially important at the end of the word. These short vowels inform us whether the words are nominative, accusative, or genitive case.

The rules for using the ending signs are quite complicated even among native speakers of Arabic.

Even though they are complicated, we still need to review them. I will make every effort to make it as simple as possible.

The short vowel signs are two kinds : the basic signs and the derived signs.

The basic signs are:

1. " fet-hah"
2. " dammeh"
3. " kasrah"
4. " sukoon"

The Derived signs are:

1. Nunation
2. Doubling
3. Nunation and Doubling

These signs will be discussed in detail following the basic signs.

A. The Short basic signs:

They are the foundation of the writing and reading rules. They go above and below the Arabic consonants and they function as vowels.

1. The "fet-hah"(˗) gives an "a" sound like cat and fat (a short vowel sound)
2. The "dammeh"(˞) gives a "u" sound like cute and mule(a short vowel sound)
3. The "kasrah" (˗) gives a "i" sound like bit and sit (a short vowel sound)
4. The "sukoon" (˚) is used when a consonant is without any vowel mark (silent)

Examples of words that have fet-<u>h</u>ah (˚):

English Translation	Pronunciation	Connected Letters	Un-Connected Letters
to eat	akala	أكَـلَ	أ كَ لَ
to leave	taraka	تَـرَكَ	تَ رَ كَ
to go out	kharaja	خَـرَجَ	خَ رَ جَ
to lie	kathaba	كَـذَبَ	كَ ذَ بَ
to live in	sakana	سَـكَنَ	سَ كَ نَ
to chop	farama	فَـرَمَ	فَ رَ مَ
to get up	naha<u>d</u>a	نَهَـضَ	نَ هَ ضَ

Examples of words that have fet-<u>h</u>ah (˚)and <u>d</u>ammeh (ˊ)

English Translation	Pronunciation	Connected Letters	Un-Connected Letters
to be increased	kathura	كَثُـرَ	كَ ثُ رَ
to be easy	sahula	سَـهُلَ	سَ هُ لَ
to be nice	<u>h</u>asuna	حَسُـنَ	حَ سُ نَ
to be heavy	thaqula	ثَقُـلَ	ثَ قُ لَ
to be great	<u>a</u>zuma	عَظُـمَ	عَ ظُ مَ
to be slow	ba<u>t</u>u-a	بَـطُءَ	بَ طُ ءَ
to be salted	malu<u>h</u>a	مَلُـحَ	مَ لُ حَ

Examples of words that have fet-hah (ﹷ) and kasrah (ﹻ)

English Translation	Pronunciation	Connected Letters	Un-Connected Letters
to be blind	ami-ya	عَمِـيَ	عَ م يَ
to gain / to profit	rabiha	رَبِـحَ	رَ بِ حَ
to be aware of	alima	عَلِـمَ	عَ لِ مَ
to be sad	hazina	حَـزِنَ	حَ زِ نَ
to be full	shabi-a	شَـبِـعَ	شَ بِ عَ
to understand	fahima	فَهِـمَ	فَ هِ مَ
to be cheep	tami-a	طَمِـعَ	طَ مِ عَ

Examples of words that have fet-hah (ﹷ), dammeh (ﹹ)and kasrah (ﹻ)

English Translation	Pronunciation	Connected	Un-Connected Letters
to be sent	bu-etha	بُعِـثَ	بُ عِ ثَ
to be raised	rufi-a	رُفِـعَ	رُ فِ عَ
to be thanked	shukira	شُـكِرَ	شُ كِ رَ
to be planted	zuri-a	زُرِعَ	زُ رِ عَ
to be written	kutiba	كُتِـبَ	كُ تِ بَ
to be swept	jurifa	جُـرِفَ	جُ رِ فَ
to be buried	dufina	دُفِـنَ	دُ فِ نَ

The four short vowel sign: sukoon (ّ)

Sukoon is a small circle above the letter, used when a letter has no vowel sign. It is the pause of the ending consonant. We can use this sign to pause and un-vowel the ending consonant whenever and wherever we want. By doing that we can avoid the error of using the wrong vowel signs while we are reading.

EXAMPLES :

English Translation	Pronunciation	Connected Letters	Un-Connected Letters
father	abb	أَبْ	أ بْ
mother	umm	أُمْ	أُ مْ
blood	damm	دَمْ	دَ مْ
to write	yaktub	يَكْتُـــبْ	يَ كْ تُ بْ
sit	ijlis	إجْلِـــسْ	إ جْ لِ سْ
bear	dub	دُبْ	دُ بْ
house	bayt	بَيْـــتْ	بَ يْ تْ

19

B. The Derived Vowel Signs

We can say that the short vowels are the original and the others are derived from them. They serve as substitutes for some unwritten consonants.

The Derived Vowel Signs:

1. The Shaddeh Sign (ّ); it doubles the consonant without writing it twice. It usually comes with a basic short vowel sign.

2. The Tanwin Signs; it occurs at the end of a noun, and it is indicated by the duplication of the final vowel symbol in the word and gives the sound of an unwritten letter:
   A. (an) if the duplicated vowel symbol is fet-hah (ً).
   B. (on) if the duplicated vowel symbol is dammeh (ٌ).
   C. (in) if the duplicated vowel symbol is kasrah (ٍ)

3. Shaddeh and Tanwin both together .

1. The Shaddeh Signs

a. Examples when sheddeh (ّ) comes with fet-hah (َ) :

English Meaning	Pronunciation	With Shaddeh	Without Shaddeh
rang	ran-na	رَنَّ	رَ نْ نَ
tightened	shad-da	شَــدَّ	شَ دْ دَ
shaken	haz-za	هَــزَّ	هَ زْ زَ
smell	sham-ma	شَــمَّ	شَ مْ مَ
counted	ad-da	عَــدَّ	عَ دْ دَ
poured	sab-ba	صَــبَّ	صَ بْ بَ
wondered	zan-na	ظَــنَّ	ظَ نْ نَ

b. Examples of shaddeh (ّ) with dammeh (ُ):

English Translation	Pronunciation	With Shaddeh	Without Shaddeh
ringing	yarun-nu	يَــرُنُّ	يَ رُ نْ نُ
to tighten	yashud-du	يَشُــدُّ	يَ شُ دْ دُ
to shake	yahuz-zu	يَهُــزُّ	يَ هُ زْ زُ
to smell	yashum-mu	يَشُــمُّ	يَ شُ مْ مُ
to count	ya<u>o</u>d-du	يَعُــدُّ	يَ عُ دْ دُ
to pour	ya<u>s</u>ub-bu	يَصُــبُّ	يَ صُ بْ بُ
to tell stories	yaqu<u>s-s</u>u	يَقُــصُّ	يَ قُ صْ صُ

c. Examples of shaddeh (ّ) with kasrah (ِ):

English Translation	Pronunciation	With Shaddeh	Without Shaddeh
to arrange	yurat-tib	يُرَتَّــب	يُ رَ تْ تِ ب
to mark or teach	yu<u>a</u>l-lim	يُعَلَّــم	يُ عَ لْ لِ م
to teach	yudar-ris	يُــدَرِّس	يُ دَ رْ رِ س
to break	yukas-sir	يُكَسِّــر	يُ كَ سْ سِ ر
to discipline	yurab-bee	يُــرَبِّي	يُ رَ بْ بِ ي
to calm	yumash-shi<u>t</u>	يُمَشِّــط	يُ مَ شْ شِ ط
to clean	yuna<u>z-z</u>if	يُنَظِّــف	يُ نَ ظْ ظِ ف

2. The Tanwin Sign

It has the value of "A" when indefinite by <u>doubling the final vowel sign</u>.

a. When there is two "fet-hah" (́) above the final letter , it gives the sound of "an" pronounced , but it is not written.

Examples:

English Translation	Pronunciation	With Tanwin	Without Tanwin
A house	daran	دَارًا	دَ ا رَ نْ
A school	madrasatan	مَدْرَسَـــة	مَدْرَسَـــتَنْ
A dog	kalban	كَلْبِـــا	كَلْبَـــنْ
A river	nahran	نَهــرًا	نَهــرَنْ
A book	kitaban	كِتَـــابِـــا	كِتَـــابَنْ
A girl	bintan	بِنْتِـــا	بِنْثَـــنْ
A summer	ṣuyfan	صَـــيْفًا	صَـــيْقَنْ

b. When there are two "dammeh" (́), above the final letter, it gives the sound of "on" pronounced , but it is not written.

Examples:

English Translation	Pronunciation	With Tanwin	Without Tanwin
A house	daron	دَارٌ	دَارُنْ
A school	madrasaton	مَدْرَسَـــة	مَدْرَسَـــتُنْ
A dog	kalbon	كَلْـــبٌ	كَلْبُـــنْ
A river	nahron	نَهــرٌ	نَهــرُنْ
A book	kitabon	كِتَـــابٌ	كِتَـــابُنْ
A girl	binton	بِنْتٌ	بِنْثُـــنْ
A summer	ṣuyfon	صَـــيْفٌ	صَـــيْقُنْ

c. When there is two "kasrah" ($_\sim$) below the final letter, it gives the sound of "in" pronounced , but it is not written.

Examples :

English Translation	Pronunciation	With Tanwin	Without Tanwin
A house	darin	دارٍ	دارِنْ
A school	madrasatin	مَدْرَسَــةٍ	مَدْرَسَـــتِنْ
A dog	kalbin	كَلْــبٍ	كَلْبِــنْ
A river	nahrin	نَهْـرٍ	نَهْـرِنْ
A book	kitabin	كِتَـــابٍ	كِتَـابِنْ
A girl	bintin	بِنْـتٍ	بِنْتِـنْ
A summer	suyfin	صَـــيْفٍ	صَـــيْفِنْ

When the Nouns and Adjectives Loose their Tanwin

As we said before, the Tanwin is the doubling of the final vowel sign in the noun when indefinite. It has the value of "A" in English. However, when the word starts with al (ال), the nouns in such cases loose their Tanwin and becomes definite. The al (ال) is equivalent of the word "the" in English.

a. Examples when the words loose the doubling of fet-hah ($^{\prime}$) and change from indefinite to definite:

English Translation	Pronunciation	definite	indefinite
The girl	al-binta	البِنْـــتَ	بِنْتـــاً
The boy	al-walada	الوَلَــدَ	وَلَــداً
The egg	al-baida	البَيْـــضَ	بَيْضـــاً
The chicken	al-dajajata	الدَجاجَـــةَ	دَجاجَـــةً
The tree	al-shajarata	الشَـــجَرَةَ	شَـــجَرَةً
The student	al-taliba	الطالِـــبَ	طالِبـــاً
The sword	al-sayfa	السَـــيْفَ	سَـــيْفاً

23

b. Examples when the words loose the doubling of dammeh (ُ) and change from indefinite to definite:

English Translation	Pronunciation	definite	indefinite
The girl	al-bintu	البِنْـــــتُ	بِنْـــتٌ
The boy	al-waladu	الوَلَــدُ	وَلَــدٌ
The egg	al-baydatu	البَيْضَــــــةُ	بَيْضَــــــةٌ
The chicken	al-dajajatu	الدَجاجَــــةُ	دَجاجَــةٌ
The tree	al-shajaratu	الشَــــجَرَةُ	شَــجَرَةٌ
The student	al-talibu	الطالِــــبُ	طالِــبٌ
The sword	al-sayfu	السَــــيفُ	سَــــيفٌ

c. Examples when the words loose the doubling of kasrah (ِ) and change from indefinite to definite:

English Translation	Pronunciation	definite	indefinite
The girl	al-binti	البِنْـــــتِ	بِنْـــتٍ
The boy	al-waladi	الوَلَــدِ	وَلَــدٍ
The egg	al-baidati	البَيْضَــــــةِ	بَيْضَــــــةٍ
The chicken	al-dajajati	الدَجاجَــــةِ	دَجاجَــةٍ
The tree	al-shajarati	الشَــــجَرَةِ	شَــجَرَةٍ
The student	al-talibi	الطالِــــبِ	طالِــبٍ
The sword	al-sayfi	السَــــيفِ	سَــــيفٍ

3. Shaddeh and Tanwin both together:

a. Examples of Shaddeh with double fet-hah (ـً) :

English Translation	Pronunciation	Shaddeh with Double fet-hah
American	amreekeyyan	أمْريكِيّـــــاً
English	Engleezeyyan	إنجْليزيّـــــاً
rich	ghaneyyan	غَنِيّـــــاً
strong	quaweyyan	قويّـــــاً
Egyptian	mesreyyan	مِصْــــريّاً
intelligent	thakeyyan	ذكِيّـــــاً
pious	taqeyyan	تَقيّـــــاً

b. Examples of Shaddeh with Double dammeh (ـٌ):

English Translation	Pronunciation	Shaddeh with Double dammeh
American	Amreekeyyon	أمْــــريكيّ
English	Engleezeyyon	إنْجلــــيزيّ
rich	ganeyyon	غَنِــــيّ
strong	qaweyyon	قَــــويّ
Egyptian	Mesreyyon	مِصْــــريّ
intelligent	thakeyyon	ذكِــــيّ
pious	takeyyon	تَقِــــيّ

c. Examples of Shaddeh with Double Kasrah (ٍّ):

English Translation	Pronunciation	Shaddeh with Double kasrah
American	Amreekeyyin	أمـــريكيٍّ
English	Engleezeyyin	إنجلــــيزيٍّ
rich	ganeyyin	غـــنيٍّ
strong	qaweyyin	قـــويٍّ
Egyptian	Miṣreyyin	مِصـــريٍّ
intelligent	thakeyyin	ذكـــيٍّ
pious	taqeyyin	تَقـــيٍّ

Lesson Seven
The Pronouns
الضَـــمائر

There are two types of personal pronouns in Arabic:
un-attached and attached pronouns.

A. <u>Un-attached Pronouns</u> الضَـــمائر المُنْفَصِــــــله

You need to remember that in the Arabic language, there is a masculine
and a feminine gender. The nouns and pronouns are either masculine or
feminine. In the next chapter, there is a discussion and examples regarding
this topic. I will use "m" for masculine and "f' for feminine.

1-Unattached pronouns regarding the <u>speaking</u> person.

I (m and f)	ana	أنـــا
we (m and f)	nahno	نَخْـــنُ

Examples:

English Translation	Pronunciation	Speaking Pronouns
I am sick .	ana mareed	أنـا مَـريضٌ .
We are all sick .	nahnu mareedoon	نَخْـــنُ مَريضْـــون
I am going .	ana thahib	أنـا ذاهِبٌ .
We are all going .	nahnu thahiboon	نَخْـــنُ ذاهِبــون .
I am coming .	ana qadim	أنـا قـــادِمٌ .
We are all coming .	nahnu qadimoon	نَخْـــنُ قـــادِمون .

2. Un-attached pronouns for the <u>present masculine</u> person.

you (one m)	anta	أنْـتَ
you (two m)	antuma	أنْتُمـا
you (three or more m)	antum	أنْتُـمْ

Examples:

English Translation	Pronunciation	M. present Pronouns
you are generous .	anta kareem	أنْـتَ كَـريمٌ .
you are both generous .	antuma kareeman	أنْتُمـا كَريمـان .
you are all generous .	antum kareemoon	أنْتُـمْ كَـريمون .
you are fair .	anta <u>a</u>dil	أنْـتَ عـادِلٌ .
you are both fair .	antuma <u>a</u>dilan	أنْتُمـا عـادِلان .
you are all fair .	antum <u>a</u>diloon	أنْتُـمْ عـادِلون .

3. Un-attached pronouns for the <u>present feminine</u> person:

you (one f)	anti	أنْـتِ
you (two f)	antuma	أنْتُمـا
you (three or more f)	antunna	أنْتُـنَّ

Examples:

English Translation	Pronunciation	F. present Pronouns
you are beautiful .	anti jameelah	أنْـتِ جَميلـةٌ .
you are both beautiful .	antuma jameelatan	أنْتُمـا جَميلَتـان .
you are all beautiful .	antunna jameelat	أنْتُـنَّ جَميـلاتٌ .
you are trustworthy .	anti aminah	أنْـتِ أمينـةٌ .
you are both trustworthy .	antuma ameenatan	أنْتُمـا أمينتـان .
you are all trustworthy .	antunna ameenat	أنْتُـنَّ أمينـاتٌ .

4. Un-attached pronouns for the <u>absent masculine</u> person.

he (one m)	huwa	هُوَ
they (two m)	huma	هُمَا
they (three or more m)	hum	هُمْ

Examples:

English Translation	Pronunciation	M. absent Pronoun
he is a writer .	huwa katib	هُوَ كاتـبٌ .
they (two) are writers .	huma katiban	هُمَا كاتِبــان .
they (three or more people) are all writers .	hum katiboon	هُمْ كـــاتِبون .
he is a man .	huwa rajul	هُوَ رَجُـلٌ .
they (two) are men .	huma rajulan	هُمَا رَجـلان .
they (three or more people) are all men .	hum rijal	هُمْ رجالٌ .

5. Un-attached pronouns for the <u>absent feminine</u> person.

she (one f)	heya	هِـيَ
they (two f)	humaa	هُمَا
they (three or more f)	hunna	هُـنَّ

Examples:

English Translation	Pronunciation	F. absent Pronoun
she is clever .	heya mahirah	هِـيَ ماهِرةٌ .
they are both clever .	humaa mahiratan	هُمَا ماهِرتــان .
they are all clever .	hunna mahirat	هُـنَّ ماهِراتٌ .
she is kind .	heya lateefah	هِـيَ لطيفــــةٌ .
they are both kind .	humaa lateefatan	هُمَا لطيفتــــان .
they are all kind .	hunna lateefat	هُـنَّ لطيفــــاتٌ .

B. Attached Pronouns الضـمائر المتصـلة

The second type of pronouns is the attached pronouns. These pronouns are:

1. Attached pronouns regarding the <u>speaking</u> person .

self (m and f)	tu	تُ
self (m and f)	ee	ى
we (plural) (m and f)	na	نـا

Examples:

English Translation	Pronunciation	Speaking Pronouns
I wrote	katabtu	كَتَبْـتُ
My pen / pencil	qalamee	قَلمـي
We wrote	katabna	كَتَبْـنـا
I broke it	kasartu	كَسَـرْتُ
My idea	fekratee	فِكْـرَتَي
We broke it	kasarna	كَسَـرْنا

2. Attached pronouns for the <u>present masculine</u> person.

you (one m)	ta or ka	تَ and كَ
you (two m)	tuma or kuma	ثَمـا and كُمـا
you (three or more m)	tum or kum	ثـمْ and كُـمْ

Examples:

English Translation	Pronunciation	M. present Pronouns
you came back (one m)	rajata	رَجَعــتَ
you came back (two m)	rajatuma	رَجَعتُمـــا
you came back (three or more m)	rajatum	رَجعتُـــمْ
your book (one m)	kitabaka	كِتابَــــكَ
your book (two m)	kitabakuma	كِتابكُمـــا
your book (three or more m)	kitabakum	كِتـــابَكُمْ

3. Attached pronouns for the <u>present feminine</u> person.

you (one f)	ti or ki	كِ and تِ
you (two f)	tuma or kuma	كُمـا and تُمـا
you (three or more f)	tunna or kunna	كُــنَّ and تُــنَّ

Examples:

English Translation	Pronunciation	F. present Pronoun
you hit (one f)	darabti	ضَـــرَبْتِ
you both hit (two f)	darabtuma	ضَـــرَبْتُما
you all hit (three or more f)	darabtunna	ضَـــرَبْتُنَّ
your book (one f)	kitabaki	كِتابَـــكِ
both of your books (two f)	kitabakuma	كِتابكُمـــا
All of your books (three or more f)	kitabakunna	كِتـــابَكنَّ

4. Attached Pronouns for the <u>absent masculine</u> person.

him/his (one m)	hu	ـهُ
them/their (two m)	huma	هُما
them/their (three or more m)	hum	هُمْ

Examples:

English Translation	Pronunciation	M. Absent Pronouns
his home (one)	baituhu	بَيْتُــــهُ
their home (two)	baituhuma	بَيْتُهُمـــا
their home (three or more)	baituhum	بَيْتُهـــمْ
his treasure (one)	kinzahu	كِنْــزَهُ
their treasure (two)	kinzahuma	كِنْزَهُمـــا
their treasure (three or more)	kinzahum	كِنْـــزَهُمْ

5. Attached Pronouns for the <u>absent feminine</u> person.

her (one f)	ha	ها
them/their (two f)	huma	هُما
them/their (three or more f)	hunna	هُـنَّ

Examples:

English Translation	Pronunciation	F. Absent Pronouns
her research (one)	bahthuha	بَحْثُهـــا
their research (two)	bahthuhuma	بَحْثُهُمـــا
their research (three or more)	bahthuhunna	بَحْثُهُـــنَّ
her country (one)	watanuha	وَطَنُهـــا
their country (two)	watanuhuma	وَطَنُهُمـــا
their country (three or more)	watanuhunna	وَطَنُهُـــنَّ

Lesson Eight
Demonstrative Pronouns
أســماء الإشـــارة

The demonstrative pronouns should agree in gender and number with the object or the person.

These pronouns are:
1-Demonstrative pronouns used for <u>near singular, dual, and plural male</u>:

English Translation	Pronunciation	Near Pronouns-M
this (one m)	hatha	<u>هذا</u>
these (two m)	hathan / hathayn	<u>هـاذين/ هاذان</u>
these (three or more m)	ha-olaa	<u>هؤلاء</u>

Examples:

English Translation	Pronunciation	Near Pronouns-M
this is a boy .	hatha walad	<u>هذا</u> ولــدٌ .
these are two boys .	hathan waladan	<u>هاذان</u> ولــدان .
these are boys . (three or more)	ha-olaa awlad	<u>هؤلاء</u> أولادٌ .
this is a doctor .	hatha tabeeb	<u>هذا</u> طبيـــبٌ .
these are two doctors .	hathayn tabeeban	<u>هـاذان</u> طبيبــــان .
these are doctors. (three or more)	ha-olaa a-tibbaa	<u>هؤلاء</u> أطبــاءٌ .

2-Demonstrative pronouns used for <u>near singular, dual, and plural female</u>.

English Translation	Pronunciation	Near Pronouns-F
this (one f)	hathihi	<u>هذِهِ</u>
these (two f)	hatayn/ hatan	<u>هـــاتَيْن/هاتـان</u>
these (three or more f)	ha-olaa	<u>هؤلاء</u>

Examples:

English Translation	Pronunciation	Near Pronouns-F
this is a girl .	hathihi bint	هذِهِ بِنـتٌ .
these are two girls .	hatan bintan	هاتـانِ بِنتـانِ .
these are girls . (three or more)	ha-olaa banat	هؤُلاء بَنـاتٌ .
this is a beautiful girl .	hathihi bint jameelah	هذِه بِنـتٌ جَميلـةٌ .
these are two beautiful girls .	hatayn bintayn jameelatyn	هـاتينِ بِنتَيـنِ جَميلتَيـنِ .
these are beautiful girls . (three or more)	ha-olaa banat jameelat	هؤُلاء بَنـاتٌ جَميـلاتٌ .

3-Demonstrative pronouns used for <u>distant person or object</u>.

English Translation	Pronunciation	Distant Pronouns
that (one m)	thalika	ذلِـكَ
those (two or more m)	ola-eka	أولائِـكَ
that (singular or plural f)	telka	تِلـكَ

Examples:

English Translation	Pronunciation	Distant Pronouns
that house is big .	thalika al-bayt kabeer	ذلِـكَ البَيـتُ كَبيـرٌ .
those boys are active . (two or more)	ola-eka al-awlad nasheetoon	أولائِـكَ الأولادُ نشـيطون .
that teacher is good .	telka al-mualemah jayyedah	تِلـكَ المعلمـةُ جَيّـدةٌ .
that man is brave .	thalika al-rajulu shujaa	ذلِـكَ الرَجُـلُ شُجـاعٌ .
those students are smart . (two or more)	ola-eka al-tullab athkeyaa	أولائِـكَ الطُـلابُ أذكيـاءٌ .
that money is a lot .	telka al-amwal katheerah	تِلـكَ الأموالُ كَثـيرةٌ .

34

Lesson Nine
Relative Pronouns
الأســـماء المَوصـــولة

1-Relative Pronouns for <u>Masculine</u>:

English Translation	Pronunciation	Relative Pronouns .M
who (singular)	al-lathee	الـذى
who (dual)	al-lathan	اللـــذان
who (plural)	al-latheen	الَـــذين

Examples:

English Translation	Pronunciation	Relative Pronouns .M
the boy who is studying is smart .	al-waladu al-lathee yadros thakey	الولـــدُ الَـــذي يَـــدرُس ذكـي .
the two boys who are studying are smart .	al-waladan al-lathan yadrosan thakeyyan	الولـــدان اللَّـــذانِ يَدرســـان ذكِيــــان .
the boys who are studying are smart (plural) .	al-awlad al-latheena yadrosoon athkeyaa	الأولاد الَـــذين يَدرســـون أذكيــــاء .

2-Relative Pronouns for <u>feminine</u>:

English Translation	Pronunciation	Relative Pronouns .F
who (singular)	al-latee	الَــتى
who (dual)	al-latan	اللتــــان
who (plural)	al-laatee	اللاتــــى

Examples:

English Translation	Pronunciation	Relative Pronouns .F
the girl who is studying is smart .	al-bint al-latee tadros thakeyyah	البنتُ الَّـتي تَـدرُس ذُكِّـيـة .
the two girls who are studying are smart .	al-bintan al-latan tadrosan thakeyyatan	البنتــان اللتــان تدرســان ذكيَّــان .
the girls who are studying are smart (plural) .	al-banat al-laatee tadrosna thakeyyat	البَنـات اللاتـي تَدرسـنَ ذكيـات .

36

Lesson Ten
Interrogative Pronouns
أسماء الإستفهام

The most common used Interrogative Pronouns are:

English Translation	Pronunciation	Interrogative Pronouns
who ?	mann	مَنْ ؟
what?	matha	ماذا ؟
how?	kayfa	كَيْفَ ؟
where?	ayna	أيْنَ ؟
why?	lema	لِمَ ؟
when?	mata	مَتى ؟
how much?\how many?	kam	كَمْ ؟
is?	hal	هَلْ ؟

Example:

English Translation	Pronunciation	Interrogative Pronouns in sentences
Who are you?	mann anta	مَنْ أنْتَ ؟
What do you want?	matha tureed	ماذا تُريـد ؟
How are you?	kayfa haluk	كَيْفَ حالـك ؟
Where were you?	ayna kunt	أيْنَ كُنْت ؟
Why did you come back?	lema rajat	لِمَ رَجَعْت ؟
When will you be back?	mata taood	مَتى تَعـود ؟
How old are you?	kam omruk	كَمْ عُمـرُك ؟
Is the doctor good?	hal al-tabeeb jayyed	هَلْ الطبيـب جَيِّـد ؟

37

Lesson Eleven
Singular, Dual, and Plural Nouns
المُفْـــرَد وَالمُثَّـــنى وَالجَمِـــع

A. The <u>singular noun</u> which is referred as al-mufrad (المُقْـــرَد) denotes for singularity and it is either masculine or feminine.

Examples:

English Translation	Pronunciation	Singular Noun
star (m)	najem	نجِـــم
star (f)	najmah	نجْمَـــة
scientist (m)	alim	عـــالِم
scientist (f)	alimah	عالِمَـــة
servant (m)	khadim	خَادِم
servant (f)	khadimah	خَادِمة
guest (m)	dayf	ضَـــيف
guest (f)	dayfah	ضَـــيفة

B. The <u>dual noun</u> which is referred as al-muthana (المُثَّـــنى) is formed by adding the two letters (ن , ا) to the singular in the Nominative case and by adding the two letters (ن , ي) in the Accusative case and Genitive case. It is either masculine or feminine.

1. Examples of the adding of (ن , ا) to the singular in the Nominative case:

English Translation	Pronunciation	Dual Noun	Nominative case Singular Noun
two orphans (m)	yateeman	يَتيمــــان	يَتيـــمٌ
two orphans (f)	yateematan	يَتيمَتـــان	يَتيمــة
two generous people (m)	kareeman	كَريمــان	كَـــريمٌ
two generous people (f)	kareematan	كَريمَتـان	كَريمَــة
two clean people (m)	nazeefan	نظيفــان	نظيـــفٌ
two clean people (f)	nazeefatan	نظيفتــان	نظيفـــة
two farmer people (m)	muzari-an	مُزارعــان	مُـزارعٌ
two farmer people (f)	mazari-atan	مُزارعَتــان	مُزارعَــة

2. Examples of the adding of (ن , ي) to the singular in the Accusative case:

English Translation	Pronunciation	Dual Noun	Accusative case Singular Noun
two mountains	jabalayn	جَبَليـــن	جبــلاً
two sides	jihatayn	جهتَيــن	جهـة
two summers	suyfayn	صَـــيفين	صـــيفاً
two civilizations	hadaratayn	حَضــــارتين	حَضــارة
two plains	sahlayn	سَــهلين	سهـلاً
two ships	safeenatayn	سَـــفينتين	سَـــفينة
two pieces of land	ardayn	أرضــين	أرضــاً

3. Examples of the adding of (ي , ن) to the singular in the <u>Genitive case:</u>

English Translation	Pronunciation	Dual noun	Genitive case Singular noun
twp patients (m)	maree<u>d</u>ayn	مَريضَـــيْن	مَـريض
two patients (f)	maree<u>d</u>atayn	مَريضَـــتَيْن	مريضـةٍ
two poor people (m)	faqeerayn	فقـــيرَيْن	فقــير
two poor people (f)	faqeeratayn	فقـــيرتَيْن	فقـــيرةٍ
two weak people (m)	<u>d</u>a-eefayn	ضَـــعيفَيْن	ضَــعيفٍ
two weak people (f)	<u>d</u>a-eefatayn	ضَـــعيفَتَيْن	ضَــعيفةٍ
two unjust people (m)	zalimayn	ظــالِمَيْن	ظــالِم
two unjust people (f)	zalimatayn	ظــالِمَتَيْن	ظالمـةٍ

C. The Plural (الجمــع) :

The <u>plural noun</u>, which is referred as al-jame<u>e</u> (الجَمِــع), expresses three or more persons or things.

There are three forms:
1. The sound plural masculine   (جَمـع مُـــذكّر ســالِم)
2. The sound plural feminine   (جَمـع مُؤنّــث ســالِم)
3. The broken plural   (جَمِـع تَكْســير)

1.a. <u>The sound plural masculine</u> is formed by adding the two letters (و , ن) to the singular in the "<u>Nominative case</u>".

Examples:

English Translation	Pronunciation	Plural Noun . M	Nominative Case/Singular Noun
publishers (m)	nashiroon	ناشِــــرون	ناشِــــرٌ
rulers (m)	hakimoon	حـــاكِمون	حـــاكِمٌ
writers (m)	katiboon	كـــاتِبون	كاتِــبٌ
students (m)	taliboon	طـــالِبون	طـالِــبٌ
swimmers (m)	sabihoon	ســـابِحون	ســـابِحٌ
bankers (m)	masrifeyyoon	مَصْـــــرِفِيّون	مَصْـــــرِفِيّ
contributors (m)	musahimoon	مُســـاهِمون	مُســـاهِمٌ

1.b. In the "<u>Accusative case</u>", the sound plural masculine is formed by adding the two letters (ي , ن) to the singular .

Examples:

English Translation	Pronunciation	Plural Noun . M	Accusative case/Singular Noun
manufacturers (m)	sani-een	صـــانِعين	صـــانِعاً
farmers (m)	fallaheen	فلاحيــــن	فلاحـــاً
dreamers (m)	halimeen	حـــالِمين	حالِمـــاً
keepers (m)	hafizeen	حـــافِظين	حافِظـــاً
engineers (m)	muhandiseen	مُهَنْدِســــين	مُهَنْدِســـاً
producers (m)	muntijeen	مُنْتِجيــــن	مُنْتِجـــاً
losers (m)	khasireen	خاسِــــرين	خاسِــــراً

41

1.c. In the "Genitive case", the sound plural masculine is formed by adding the two letters (ي , ن) to the singular .

Examples:

English Translation	Pronunciation	Plural Noun . M	Genitive Case/Singular Noun
travelers (m)	musafireen	مُسَـــافِرين	مُسَـــافِر
ill (m)	mareedeen	مَريضَـــين	مَــريض
active (m)	nasheeteen	نَشِـــــيطين	نَشِـــيطِ
happy (m)	masrooreen	مَسْـرورين	مَسْـرور
engineers (m)	muhandiseen	مُهَندِسِـــين	مُهَـــندِس
oppressed (m)	mazloomeen	مَظْلــــومين	مَظْلـــوم
unjust (m)	zalimeen	ظــالِمين	ظــالِم

2.a. The sound plural feminine is formed by adding the two letters (تّ , ا) to the singular in the "Nominative case" with two dammeh at the end.

Examples:

English Translation	Pronunciation	Plural Noun .F	Nominative Case/Singular Noun
doctors (f)	tabeebatun	طَبيبـــاتٌ	طَبيبَـــــة
ill (f)	mareedatun	مَريضـــاتٌ	مَريضَـــة
wise (f)	hakeematun	حَكيمـــاتٌ	حَكيمَـــة
happy (f)	masrooratun	مَسْـــرورْاتٌ	مَسْـــرورَة
players (f)	la-ebatun	لاعِبـــاتٌ	لاعِبَـــة
active (f)	nasheetatun	نَشِـــــيطاتٌ	نَشِـــيطة
coming (f)	qadimatun	قادِمـــاتٌ	قادِمَـــة

42

2.b. In the "<u>Accusative case</u>", the sound plural feminine is formed by adding the two letters (تٍ , ا) with two kasreh at the end to the singular .

Examples:

English Translation	Pronunciation	Plural Noun. F	Accusative Case/Singular Noun
tall (f)	ṭaweelatin	طـــويلاتٍ	طويلــــة
beautiful (f)	jameelatin	جَميـــلاتٍ	جَميلــة
doctors (f)	ṭabeebatin	طبيبــــاتٍ	طبيبــــة
repenters (f)	ta-ebatin	تائبــــاتٍ	تائبــــة
researchers (f)	baḥithatin	باحثـــاتٍ	باحثـــة
scholars (f)	a-limatin	عالِمــاتٍ	عالمـة
models (f)	a-riḍatin	عارضـــاتٍ	عارضَـــة

2.c. In the "<u>Genitive case</u>", the sound plural feminine is formed by adding the two letters (تٍ , ا) with two kasreh at the end to the singular .

Examples:

English Translation	Pronunciation	PLural Noun .F	Genitive Case/Singular Noun
doctors (f)	ṭabeebatin	طبيبــــاتٍ	طبيبــــةٍ
short (f)	qaṣeeratin	قصـــيراتٍ	قصــــيرَةٍ
teachers (f)	mual-limatin	مُعَلَّمــــاتٍ	مُعَلَّمَــــةٍ
energetic (f)	nasheeṭatin	نشـــيطاتٍ	نشــــيطةٍ
tough (f)	shadeedatin	شَـــديداتٍ	شَـــديدَةٍ
writers (f)	katibatin	كاتبَـــاتٍ	كاتبَـــةٍ
tall (f)	ṭaweelatin	طـــويلاتٍ	طويلـــةٍ

43

3. The third form of plural is "<u>Broken Plural</u>" (جَمِــع تَّكْـــــــير), which is formed by changing the singular to plural irregularly, whether the noun is feminine or masculine.

Examples:

English Translation	Pronunciation	Broken Plural Noun	Singular Noun
homeland	awṭan	أوْطـانْ	وَطَـنْ
men	rijal	رجـالْ	رَجُـلْ
gardens	hada-ik	حَـــدائقْ	حَديقـه
schools	madaris	مَـدارسْ	مَدْرَسـة
pens	aqlam	أقـلامْ	قَلَــمْ
red	humur	حُمُـرْ	أحْمَـرْ
groups	firaq	فِـــرَقْ	فِرْقـة

Lesson Twelve
Gender
المــذكر والمؤنــث

Arabic nouns are divided into two categories: Masculine and Feminine; whether it is a person, an animal, or an object.

The masculine noun does not require any gender sign.

Examples:

Pronunciation	Arabic Name . M
Yousef	يوســف
Adnan	عَـدنان
Mohammed	محمد

A Feminine noun on the other hand has a Feminine sign .These signs are as follows :

a) Closed 'ta' at the end (ة).

Examples:

English Translation	Pronunciation	Arabic Word . F
cow	baqarah	بَقـــرة
table	tawelah	طاولــة
a female name	ra-eda	رائـدة

45

b) The Elongated alif (ا) with a hamza (ء) at the end.

Examples:

English Translation	Pronunciation	Arabic Word . F
electricity	kahrubaa	كَهْرُبـــاء
green	kha<u>d</u>raa	خَضْــراء
desiring	rajaa	رَجـاء

c) The short alif at the end.

Examples:

English Translation	Pronunciation	Arabic Word . F
person's name	salwa	سَـــلوى
candy	<u>h</u>alwa	حَــوى
person's name	fadwa	فَــدوى

Sometimes the feminine noun does not have a feminine sign.

Examples:

English Translation	Pronunciation	Arabic Word . F
a female name	mariam	مَـــريَم
a female name	fatin	فــاتِن
a female name	sa<u>h</u>ar	سَـحر

We should know that the gender of the adjective or the gender of the verb always follows the same gender of their subjects.

46

Lesson Thirteen
The Nominal Sentence
الجُمْلــة الإســـميَّة

The Nominal Sentence always starts with a noun. The nominal sentence in Arabic consists of two nouns:

Subject (mubtadaa-مُبْتَــدَأ) and predicate (khabar-خَبَــر), which tells something about the subject and completes the sentence. They are both in the nominative case with a <u>d</u>ammeh sign (ُ).

The predicate always agrees with its subject in respect of gender and number, except when the subject is a plural object, not a person, the predicate will be a singular feminine as it appears in the seventh example.

Generally, the subject would be definite by adding the (al- ال) at the beginning which means "the" and makes it a definite noun. The predicate is always indefinite.

Examples:

English Translation	Pronunciation	Nominal Sentence
The manufacturer is skillful .	al-<u>s</u>ani-<u>o</u> mahiron	الصـــانعُ مــاهرٌ.
The girl is beautiful .	al-bintu jameelaton	البِنْـــتُ جَميلــةٌ.
The men are strong .	al-rijalu aqweyaa-on	الرجــالُ أقويــاءٌ.
The ladies are nice .	al-nisa-o lateefaton	النِســـاءُ لطيفـــاتٌ.
The knowledge is a guiding light .	al-<u>e</u>lmo nooron	العِلــــمُ نـورٌ.
The two gardens are blooming .	al-<u>h</u>adeekatan mozhiratan	الحـــديقتان مُزْهِرتَــان.
The streets are clean .	al-shawari<u>o</u> na<u>z</u>eefaton	الشَـــوارعُ نظيفــةٌ.

47

Lesson Fourteen
The Construct Phrase
المُضــاف وَالمُضــاف إليــه

As we said before , the nominal sentence consists of a subject and a predicate. The subject sometimes consists of two nouns, one follows the other immediately. These two nouns have some kind of relationship,an ownership relation, a blood relation, or the second noun maybe the doer or object of the first noun, or any other type of relationship.

The first noun which is called (mudaf-مُضــاف) would be indefinite, so it comes without the definite article (al- ال) and can be in any grammatical case depending on its function in the sentence.

The second noun which is called (mudaf elaih-مُضــاف إليــه), on the other hand, it is always in the genitive case with a kasrah at the end.

We should remember that if the "mudaf noun" is a dual(مُثنَّـــى) or sound plural form (جَمـــع مذكر سالم), it loses its final (ن), as in the second and third examples.

Examples:

English Translation	Pronunciation	The Construct Phrase
Fasting in Ramadan is beneficial .	sawmu Ramadana mofeed	صَــوْمُ رَمَضــان مُفيــد.
The baby's eyes are innocent .	ayna al-tifil baree-atan	عَيْنــا الطِفْــل بَريئتــان.
The car drivers are in a hurry .	sa-e-qoo al-sayyarat mostajiloon	ســائِقو السَــيّارات مُسْــتَعْجِلون.
Loving God is a glory .	hobbu Allahi ezz	حُــبُّ اللـةِ عِز.
Respecting the elderly is an obligation .	ihtiramu al-kabeer wajib	إحْتِـــرامُ الكَبـــير واجب.
Mohammad's shirt is clean .	qameesu Mohammed nazeef	قَمِــصُ مُحَمَّــدٍ نظيــف .
People on earth are responsible .	ahlu al-arrd mas-ooloon	أهلُ الأرضِ مَسْــؤُولون.

Lesson Fifteen
the Adjective
الصِـــفة

The adjective الصِـــفة is a word that comes after a noun to describe that noun , which is called the qualified noun موصـوف .

The adjective agrees with the qualified noun in cases of declension, gender, number, definiteness, and indefiniteness, except in one case, if the qualified noun is plural place, or a plural object masculine or feminine , its adjective would be feminine singular as in the sixth example.

Examples:

English Translation	Pronunciation	adjective in sentences
This book is beneficial .	hatha kitabon mufeedon	هَذا كِتَـــابٌ مُفيـــدٌ.
I saw two beautiful houses .	ra-aito baytayni jameelayni	رأيــتُ بَيْتَيْـــــنِ جَميلَيْـــــنِ.
Those men are strong.	ha-ola-e rejalon aqweyaa	هؤلاء رجـالٌ أقْويــــاءٌ.
I smelled the beautiful rose .	shamamtu al-wardata al-jameelata	شَـــمَمْتُ الـــوَرْدَة الجَميلَـــــة.
Those two engineers are clever .	hatan mohandisatan thakeyyatan	هاتـان مُهَنْدِسَــــتان ذَكِيَّتَـــــان.
The deep seas are majestic .	al-biharo al-ameeqato azeematon	البحـــارُ العَميقَـــة عَظيمــة.
Safa is a sincere girl.	safa bintun mukhlisah	صَــفا بِنْــتٌ مُخْلِصَـــــة.

49

Lesson Sixteen
Kana and it's Sisters
كـانَ وَأَخَواتِهــا

Kana (كان) and its categories are verbs that are incomplete. Ordinary verbs denote both action and time. However, these incomplete verbs, indicate time but with no action.

When kana (كان) or any of its sisters are added to the beginning of a nominal sentence, it causes the first word to be in the nominative case and called the noun of kana . The second word will be in the accusative case and called the predicate of cana .

The list of kana (كان) and its most common sisters:

English Translation	Pronunciation	Kana and its Categories
to be	kana	كـانَ
to become	sara	صـارَ
not to be	laysa	لَيـــسَ
to become at dawn	asbaha	أصـــبَحَ
to become in the evening	amsa	أمـســى
to become in the afternoon	adha	أضـحـى
to remain	zalla	ظـلَّ
to become during the night	bata	بـاتَ
to continue	ma zala	ما زالَ
as long as	ma dama	ما دامَ

NOTE:

Each verb can be converted to the present tense (mu<u>d</u>ar<u>e</u>-ع مُضـــارع)
imperative (amir-ْأمـر) and active participle (isim fa<u>e</u>l- إسِـم فاعِــل) except for
the verb (laysa-َلَيْـــس) and (ma dama-َمـادام).

Examples:

English Translation	Pronunciation	Kana and its Categories in Sentences
The house was clean .	kana al-baytu na<u>z</u>eefan	كـانَ البيــتُ نظِيفــاً.
The cold became nippy .	<u>s</u>ara al-bardu qari<u>s</u>an	صـارَ البَــرْدُ قارصـاً.
The situation is not easy .	laysa al-amru hayyenan	لَيْـسَ الأمْـرُ هيّنـاً.
The water became frozen (in the morning) .	a<u>s</u>ba<u>h</u>a al-ma-o jamidan	أصْـبَحَ المـاءُ جامِـداً.
The poor man became hungry (in the evening)	amsa al-faqeeru ja-e-<u>an</u>	أمْسـى الفقـيرُ جائِعـاً .
The traveler became exhausted in the afternoon .	a<u>dh</u>a al-mosafiru mot-<u>q</u>ban	أضْـحى المُسـافِرُ مُتْعَبـاً.
The soldier remained steady .	<u>z</u>alla al-jondeyyu thabitan	ظـلَّ الجُنْـدِيّ ثابتـاً.

Lesson Seventeen
Inna and its Sisters
إنَّ وَأَخَواتهــا

Inna and its categories are particles. Each particle has a specific meaning. When they are added to a nominal sentence, the meaning of the sentence changes and also the subject of the sentence changes from the nominative to the accusative case.

The first word of the nominal sentence is called, the noun of inna or any of its category. The second word is called the predicate of inna and it remains in the nominative case.

The list of (inna- إنّ) and its most common sisters:

English Translation	Pronunciation	Inna and its Categories
surely, certainly	inna	إنَّ
that	anna	أنَّ
is like, as if	ka-anna	كــانَّ
however, but	la-kinna	لكِــنَّ
I wish that, if only	layta	لَيْــتَ
I hope, perhaps	la-ala	لَعَــلَّ

Examples:

English Translation	Pronunciation	Inna and its Categories in Sentences
Surely the mosquitoes are a lot .	inna al-ba-ooda katheeron	إنَّ البَعـوضَ كَثـــيرٌ .
I am glad that the rain is heavy .	yasorronee anna al-shitaa ghazeeron	يَسُـــرني أنَّ الشِـــتاءَ غَـزيرٌ .
The moon was like a lamp .	ka-anna al-qamara misbahon	كَــأنَّ القَمَـــرَ مِصــباحٌ .
The wind is strong but the weather is warm .	al-hawa-o shadeed lakinna al-jawwa dafi-on	الهَــواء شَـــديدٌ لكِـــنَّ الجَــوَّ دافِــئٌ .
I wish that the spring is nearby .	layta al-rabeega qareebon	لَيْـــتَ الـــرَّبيعَ قَريـــبٌ .
Perhaps the news is true .	la-alla al-khabara saheehon	لَعَــلَّ الخَبَـــرَ صَـــحيحٌ .

Lesson Eighteen
The Verbal Sentence
الجُمْلَـــــة الفِعْلِيَـــــة

The verbal sentence is a sentence which begins with a verb. The majority of the Arabic verbs consist of three root . There are some other verbs consist of four letters or root . However, they are less in numbers.

From the verbal root we can form other verbs and nouns by adding one, two, or three letters to the three root or to the four root , these letters are then called the letters of increase .The verb (fa-ala -فَعَـــلَ) and its derivatives are used as patterns in Arabic grammar books.

The verbs is divided into three categories:

1) The perfect verb or the past tense (فِعِـــلْ ماضِي)
2) The imperfect verb or the present tense (فِعِـــل مُضـــارِع)
3) The imperative verb or command verb (فِعِـــلْ أَمِـرْ)

1) the Perfect Verb or the Past Tense الفِعــــل الماضــــي

The perfect verb is the verb that happened in the past and is called perfect because the action is finished before the time of speaking.

The perfect verb is the verb that consist of three letters or root from which the imperfect verb and imperative verb are formed. It usually comes in the accusative case.

The vowel of the first and third letter of the simple past tense is always the fet-hah vowel (ﹷ) . However , the vowel of the middle letter may be either a fet-hah (فَعَـــلَ), a dammeh (فَعُـــلَ) or kasrah (فَعِـــلَ) . We should know that the verb agrees with the subject in gender only if the verb precedes the subject as it appears in the first four examples.

However, the verb agrees with the subject in gender and in number when the subject comes before the verb and will have the suitable accusative sign at the end. This is illustrated in the last three examples.

Examples :

English Translation	Pronunciation	Perfect verbs in sentences
The boy sat down .	jalasa al-waladu	جَلَسَ الوَلَـدُ.
The two guards heard the sound .	same-a al-harisan al-sawt	سَمِعَ الحارسـان الصَـوْت.
The time is almost over .	qaroba al-waqtu min al-intihaa	قـرُبَ الوَقـتُ مِنَ الإنتِهـاء.
The merchants closed their shops.	aghlaqa al-tujjar dakakeenahum	أغْلَـقَ التُجـارُ دكــاكينَهُمْ.
The patient left from the hospital .	al-mareedatu kharajat min al-mustashfa	المَريضَـة خَرَجَـت مِـن المُسْتَشْـفى.
The two riders got off from the bus .	al-rakiban nazala min al-bas	الراكِبــان نـزَلا مِنَ البـاص.
The travelers arrived at the airport.	al-musafirat wasalna ela al-matar	المُســافِراتُ وَصَـلنَ إلـى المَطـار.

2. The Imperfect Verb or Present Tense الفِعِــــــل المُضـــــارِع

The imperfect verb is the verb that is incomplete in action . The action of this verb is still happening at the present time and it is on going . It is formed by adding one or more of these letters (أ , ت , ن , ي) to the past tense, and applying a sukoon (ْ) to the second consonant of the verb.

1. The hamzeh (أ) is used if the subject is a singular <u>speaking</u> person. Examples, (دَرَس) →(أَدْرُسُ), I am studying.

2. The ta (ت) is used if the subject is a <u>present</u> person. Example, (دَرَسَ) → (تَـــدْرُسُ), you are studying.

3. The ya (ي) is used if the subject of the verb is a <u>absent</u> person. Example, (دَرَسَ)→(يَـــدْرُسُ), he is studying.

4. The na (ن) is used if the subject is <u>a plural speaking</u> person. Example, (دَرَسَ)→(نَـــدْرُسُ), we are studying.

Note :
The imperfect verb agrees with the subject in gender, if the verb precedes the subject as it appears in the following first three examples .

In addition , the verb agrees with the subject in gender and number if the subject comes before the verb as it appears in the forth and fifth examples. The Imperfect verb could give the meaning of the future tense if we add the word (sawfa - سَـــوْفَ) or the particles (س) before the present verb as it appears in the sixth and seventh examples.

Examples:

English Translation	Pronunciation	Present Verb in Sentences
Yousef wakes up early .	yastayqizu Yousef bakiran	يَسْـــــــــتَيقِظ يوسـف بـــاكِراً.
The sun rises in the morning .	toshriqu al-shamsu fee al-<u>s</u>aba<u>h</u>	تُشْـــــرِقُ الشَـــمسُ فـي الصَـــباح.
The soldiers preserve the peace .	yo<u>h</u>afizu al-jonood <u>g</u>lla al-amin	يُحـــــافِظ الجُنــــودُ علـى الأمِـن.
The moon appears at night .	al-qamaru ya<u>z</u>haru laylan	القمَـــــرُ يَظهـــرُ لَيْـــــلاً.
The two dogs guarded the farm .	al-kalban ya<u>h</u>rosan al-mazra-<u>gh</u>	الكَلبـــــان يَحرُسَـــان المَزرَعَـــة.
I will study .	sawfa adrosu	سَــوفَ أدْرُسُ.
I will study .	sa-adrosu	سَــأدْرُسُ.

3. The Imperative or the Command Verb فِعِـــــل الأمِـر

The Imperative verb means to command someone to do something (positive command) as it appears in the first four examples, or not to do something(negative command) by adding the particle (لا) before the command verb as it appears in the fifth to seventh examples.

The Imperative verb is formed from the Present verb by removing the first letter and replacing it with hamzeh (أ) with a <u>d</u>ammeh (ُ) or a kasrah vowel

(ِ). Then add a sukoon (ْ) to the last latter.

Examples:

English Translation	Command Verb	Present Verb
study!	odros / أُدْرُسْ	تَـــدْرُسُ
hear!	esma / اسْـــمَعْ	تَسْـــمَعُ

However, if the second letter , of the present verb is with the vowel sign, then we drop the first letter of the present verb and we add a sukoon (ْ) to the last letter.

Examples:

English Translation	Command Verb	Present Verb
weigh!	zen / زِنْ	يَــزِنُ
promise!	ed / عِد	يَعِــدُ

Examples of command verbs in sentences :

English Translation	Pronunciation	Command Verb in Sentences
Go to school early !	ithhab ela al-madrasati mobukkiran	اذهَبْ إلى المَدْرَسَــةِ مُبَكِّــراً.
Respect the rules at school !	hafi-zee ala al-nizam fee al-madrasah	حــافِظِي عَلــى النِظــام فــي المَدْرَسَــةِ.
Drink the delicious juice !	ishraba al-aseer al-latheeth	اشْـــرَبِا العَصِــير اللذيــذّ.
Support the oppressed !	onsoroo al-mazloom	أنصُـــروا المَظْلــــومْ.
Don't play with the medicine .	la talab bildawaa	لا تَلْعَـــبْ بالــدَواءْ.
Don't pluck out the roses .	la taqtifa al-ward	لا تَقطِفِــــا الــوَرْدِ.
Don't laugh out loud .	la tad-hakna bi-sawtin alen	لا تَضْــــحَكْنَ بصَــــوْتٍ عـالٍ.

57

Lesson Nineteen
Nouns which are Derived from the Verbal Root
أســماء مشـــتقة من الفعـــل الثلاثـــي

As we mentioned before, the verb (fa-ala-فَعَـــلَ) is in the past tense and its derivatives (the present and command verb) are used as patterns to form some nouns by adding one, two, or three letters to the three root or to the four root.

Some of the nouns which are derived from the verbal root are:

1. The "Active Participle" which denotes the agent or doer of an action.
   (ism al-fa-el - اسـم الفاعِـــل).

2. The "Passive Participle" which conveys the sufferer of an action.
   (ism al-maf-ool- اسِـــمْ المَفعـــول).

3. The noun of "time and place".
   (ism al-zaman wa-al-makan- اسِـمْ الزَمَـــان وَالمَكـــان)

4. The noun of " Instruments"
   (ism al-aleh- اسِـمْ الآلَـــة   )

5. The noun of "Comparative".
   (ism al-tafdeel- اسِـمْ التَفضـــــيلْ   )

1. Active Participle اسِـمْ الفاعِـــل

It denotes the agent or the person who does the action . The pattern of the active participle is (fa-el-فاعِـــلْ) if it is derived from the past tense (fa-ala- فَعَـــلَ). The first four examples expresses this concept . However, if the verb is in the present tense, the active participle is formed by replacing the first letter with the letter ma (م) with a dammeh vowel (ُ) and applying a kasrah (ِ) to the second letter from the end of the verb. This concept is illustrated in the last two examples .

58

Examples:

English Translation	Pronunciation	Active Participle
I think the witness is honest .	azonnu al-shahida sadeq	أَظُنُّ الشَّـــاهِدَ صَـــادِقْ.
Perhaps the burglar is regretful .	la-alla al-sariqa nadim	لَعَـــلَّ السَّـــارِقَ نَـــادِمْ.
I thought the crescent moon is absent .	zanantu al-hilala gha-eb	ظَنَنْـــتُ الهِـــلالَ غائِـــب.
The plate was empty .	kana al-sahnu farigh	كـــانَ الصَّـــحْنُ فَـــارِغْ.
I saw the fruitful trees .	ra-aito al-shajara mothmir	رَأَيْـــتُ الشَّـــجَرَ مُثْمِـــرْ.
The worshipper continues to repent .	la yazal al-a-bidu mostaghfer	لا يَـــزال العابِـــدُ مُسْـــتَغْفِرْ.
I know that the teacher is sincere	aarif anna al-mo-allima mokhles	أَعْـــرِفْ أَنَّ المعلــمَ مُخْلِـــصْ.

2. The Passive Participle   اسِـــمْ المَفْعـــــــول

The passive participle expresses the sufferer of an action. There are two patterns that are formed. It can be derived from the past tense or the present tense.

The passive participle which is derived from the past tense (fa-al-فَعَــل) becomes (maf-ool-مَفعـــول). The first four examples expresses this concept.

The passive participle which is derived from the present tense is formed by replacing the first letter with the letter (ma- م) with a dammeh vowel (مُ) and applying a fet-ha vowel to the second letter from the end of this present verb. Examples of this concept is expressed in the last three examples.

Examples:

English Translation	Pronunciation	Passive Participle
The door is still open .	ma zala al-babu maftooh	ما زالَ البـــابُ مَفْتـــوح.
I believe the lesson is understood	a-zunnu al-darsa mafhoom	أَظُـــنُّ الـــدَرْسَ مَفْهـــوم.
I found the box broken .	wajadtu al-sondooqa maksoor	وَجَـــدتُ الصُّـــندوقَ مَكْســـور.
The poor slept deprived .	amsa al-faqeeru mahroom	أَمْســـى الفَقــيرُ مَحْـــروم.
I left the store organized .	taraktu al-dukkana murattab	تَرَكْـــتُ الـــدُّكانَ مُرَتَّـــب.
I found the guest treated with hospitality .	wajadtu al-dayfa mukram	وَجَـــدتُ الضَّـــيْفَ مُكْـــرَم.
Talking less is desired .	al-kalamu al-qaleel mustahsan	الكَـــلام القَلــيل مُسْتَحْسَـــن.

3. Noun of Time or Place اســم الزَمـــان أو المَكـــان

The noun of place or time expresses the time or place of an action. There are two patterns that are formed. It is derived from the past or the present tense.

The noun of place or thing is in the form of (maf-al- مَفْعَـــل) when it is formed from the past tense (fa-ala- فَعَـــلَ) this is illustrated in the first four examples .

When the noun of place or thing is derived from the present tense (yaf-ol- يَفْعُـــل), it is in the form of (maf-el- مَفْعِـــل). This is illustrated in the last three examples.

English Translation	Pronunciation	Nouns of Time or Place
The garden entrance is wonderful .	madkhalu al-ḥadeeqati badee	مَـدْخَل الحديقــة بَــديع.
The village exit is narrow .	makhragu al-qaryati ḍayyiq	مَخْــرَج القرْيَـــةِ ضَـــيّقٌ.
The restaurant in town is clean .	maṭamu al-madeenati naẓeef	مَطْعَــم المَدينـــةِ نظيــف.
The director's office is spacious .	maktab al-modeer wasi-e	مَكْتَــب المُــدير واسِـــع.
The bus station is near .	mawqif al-baṣat qareeb	مَوْقِـــف الباصــات قريـــب.
The sunset is beautiful .	magribu al-shamsi jameel	مَغْــرِب الشَـــمْس جَميـــل.
The water source is pure .	mawridu al-maa ṣafee	مَــوْرِد المـاء صـافي.

4. Noun of Instrument   اســم الآلـــة

The noun of instrument expresses the instrument that is used for the action. There are two patterns that are formed. It is derived from the past or present tense.

The noun of instrument that is formed from the past tense (fa-ala- فَعَـــلَ) is (mef-aalon- مِفْعَـــالٌ) as in the first and second example and (mef-alah- مِفْعَلـــة) as in the third and fourth example .

On the other hand the noun of instrument is (mif-al- مِفْعَـــل) when it is formed from the present tense (yaf-al- يَفْعَـــل)as in the last three examples.

English Translation	Pronunciation	Noun of Instrument
The guard opened the door with the key .	fataha al-harisu al-baba belmiftah	فَتَحَ الحَارِسُ البَابَ بِالمِفْتَاح.
The farmer cultivated the land with the plow .	haratha al-fallahu al-arda belmihrath	حَرَثَ الفَلاَّحُ الأرْضَ بِالمِحْرَاث.
The boy licked the food with the spoon .	la-qqa al-waladu al-akla belmil-qqati	لَعِقَ الوَلَدُ الأكْلَ بِالمِلعَقَةِ.
The hunter hunted the bird with a trap .	sada al-sayyadu al-tayra belmisyadati	صَادَ الصَّيَّادُ الطيْرَ بِالمِصْيَدَةِ.
My mother sewed the dress with a needle .	khatat um-mee al-thawba belmikhyet	خاطت أمي الثَّوْبَ بِالمِخْيَط.
I directed the vehicle with the steering wheal .	qudtu al-sayyarah belmiqwed	قُدْتُ السَيَّارة بِالمِقْوَد.
The blacksmith uses a file in his work .	yastamel al-haddad al-mebred fe amalehi	يَسْتَعْمِل الحَدَّاد المِبْرَد فـي عمله.

5. The Noun of Comparative اسـم التَّفْضِيل

The noun of comparative expresses that the two persons or things participate in a common quality, however, one of them surpasses the other with more quality.

There is only one pattern that is formed which is (af-al- أفْعَل). here are seven examples to illustrate this concept.

English Translation	Pronunciation	Noun of Comparative
The elephant is bigger than the horse .	al-feelu akbaru men al-hisan	الفِيلُ أكْبَرُ مِنَ الحصَان.
The palace is more beautiful than the house .	al-qasru ajmalu men al-bayt	القصْرُ أجْمَلُ مِنَ البَيْت.
Natalia is older than Noor .	natalia akbaru men noor	نتاليا أكْبَرُ مِن نـور.
The knowledge is more beneficial than money .	al-elmu anfa-o men al-mal	العِلْمُ أنْفَعُ مِن المال.
The knowledgeable person is better than the ignorant one .	al-alimo afda-lo men al-jahil	العَالِمُ أفضَلُ مِن الجاهِل.
The repentant is better than the sinner .	al-ta-ibu ahsanu men al-asee	التائِبُ أحسنُ مِن العاصِي.
The man is stronger than the boy .	al-rajulo aqwa men al-walad	الرَجُـلُ أقوى مِن الوَلَـد.

Lesson Twenty
The Particles
الحــروف

A particle is a word which does not convey a sense on its own . However, it contributes to the meaning of the sentence.

There are many types of particles. Some of the Particles effect the grammatical case of the word. Among these types are:

1) Prepositions (<u>h</u>oroof al-jur- حروف الجــر)

2) Conjunctions (<u>h</u>oroof al-<u>at</u>if- حروف العطــف)

The particles that do not effect the grammatical case of the word. Among these types are:

1) Interjections (<u>h</u>oroof al-nidaa- حروف النـــداء)

2) Interrogatives (<u>h</u>oroof al-estifham- حروف الإســـتفهام)

1)Prepositions حروف الجــر

Prepositions (حروف الجـر) are particles used with a noun to show its relation to some other word in the sentence and it causes the noun to be in the Genitive case.

The preposition are either :

a . Separable as in the first five examples .
b . Inseparable as in the last three examples .

Here are some common prepositions:

English Translation	Pronunciation	Prepositions
in (time or place)	fee	فـي
of, from	menn	مِن
to, until	ela	إلـى
about, from, of	ann	عَن
on, above, over	ala	عَلـى
like, as	ka	كَ
for, to	la	لَ
by, with	ba	بَ

Examples :

English Translation	pronunciation	Preposition in sentences
The food is in the refrigerator .	al-taamu fee al-thallajati	الطعـامُ فـي الثلاجَـةِ .
I came back from the marketplace .	ataytu min al-sowqi	أتيْـتُ مِـن السـوق .
I listened to the advice .	istamatu ela al-naseehati	اسْـتَمَعتُ إلـى النصـيحَةِ .
Forgive who apologizes .	isfah an al-mootathir	إصـفَح عَنْ المُعْتَـذِر .
The food is on the table .	al-aklu ala al-tawilati	الأكـلُ عَلـى الطاولَـةِ .
The green plums are sour like lemons .	al-karazu hamidon kal-laymooni	الكَـرَزْ حـامِضّ كـاللَيْمونِ .
I listened to the announcer .	istamatu lil-muthee	اسْـتَمَعتُ للمُـذيع .
I accepted the situation .	radeytu bil-amri	رَضِـيْتُ بـالأمرِ .

2) Conjunctions   حروف العطـف

Conjunctions are particles used to unite two nouns or two verbs. The second noun or verb always takes the same vowel of the first one.

The conjunctions are either :

a . Separable as in the first six examples .
b . Inseparable as in the last two examples .

Here are some common conjunctions:

English Translation	Pronunciation	Conjunctions
or	amm	أم
or	aw	أو
and then	thumma	ثُمَّ
but	la-kenn	لكـنْ
even more	hatta	حَتَّـى
not	la	لا
and	wa	و
then	fa	ف

Examples :

English Translation	Pronunciation	Conjunctions in sentences
Did you study science or math?	adarasta al-oloom am al-hisab	أدَرَسْتَ العُلـومَ أم الحسـاب ؟
Eat honey or dates .	kol asalan aw tamran	كُـلْ عَسَـلاً أو ثمـراً .
We planted the wheat then we harvested it .	zarana al-qamih thumma hasadnahu	زرَعْنـا القمـح ثُـمَّ حَصَـدْناهُ .
The president didn't come but the vice president came .	ma jaa al-masool lakin na-ebuhu	ما جاءَ المسـؤول لكـنْ نائبُـهُ
The teacher was late and so was the principle .	ta-akhara al-modarrisu hatta al-mudeer	تـأخَرَ المُـدَرِّسُ حَتَّـى المُـدير .
I broke the glass and not the plate .	kasartu al-kasa la al-sahna	كَسَـرْتُ الكـأسَ لا الصَـحْنَ .
I like lemons and oranges .	ohibbu al-laimoon wa al-burtuqal	أحِبُ الليْمـونَ والبرتقـال .
The summer came and the plants grew .	jaa al-sayfu fanadja al-zaro	جاءَ الصَـيفُ فنَضَـجَ الـزَرعُ .

64

Other Types of Common Particles

1) Interjections particles حروف النـــداء

-oh (ya - يـا) example :
(ya tilmeeth - يـا تِلميـــــذ) Oh, student !
-oh (ya ay-yuha - يـا أيُّهـا) example :
(ya ayyuha al-talameeth- يـا أيُّهـا التَّلاميـــــذ) Oh, students!

2) Interrogative particles حروف الإســـــتفهام

- have (hal - هَل) example :
(hal darasta - هَل دَرَســـت) Have you studied?
- did (ah- أ) example :
(a-darasta- أَدَرَســـت) Did you study?

3) The Answer particles حُروف الجَـــواب

- yes (nam - نَعَـــم) example :
(nam ya abee - نَعَـــم يـا أبــي) Yes, oh my father .
- no (la - لا) example :
(la ya abee - لا يـا أبــي)- No, oh my father .

4) The particles: qad قَــدْ and ma ما

the particles (qad - قَــدْ) is used with past tense to give the meaning of the "near past" example :
(qad darasa- قَــدْ دَرَس) He has studied .

The particle (ma- ما) is used with the past tense to give the meaning of "the negative past" example :
(ma darasa - ما دَرَسَ)   He did not study .

5) The particles: sawfa سَــوْفَ and sa س
these two particle are used with the present verb to change it to the "future tense".

The particle (sawfa - سَـوف) is used for the "distant future".

example :

(sawfa adros - سَـــوْفَ أدْرُسْ)   I will study .

The particle (sa - س) indicates "near future" example :

(sa-adros - ســأدرُس) I would study .

Appendix A
Common Phrases

English Translation	Pronunciation	In Arabic
Hello	marhaba	مَرحَبـا
Welcome	ahlan	أهـلاً
How are you !	kaif halok	كيـف حالـك ؟
Good	be-khair	بخـير
What is your name ?	ma ismak	ما إسمك ؟
My name is ...	ismee...	إسـمي ...
Where are you from ?	min ayna anta	مِن أيـن أنـتَ ؟
I am from ...	ana min ...	أنـا مِن ...
What is your job ?	matha tamal	ماذا تَعمَـل ؟
Where is the bathroom ?	ayna al-ham-mam	أيـن الحَمـام ؟
I am hungry !	ana jowan	أنـا جوعان !
Where is the food ?	ayna al-ta-am	أيـن الطعـام ؟
I am sleepy !	ana nasan	أنـا نعسـان!
I am thirsty !	ana atshan	أنـا عَطشـان!
Where is the hotel ?	ayna al-funduq	أيـن الفنـدُق ؟
I need a taxi .	ureed taxi	أريـد تَكسـي .
I need to go to the airport .	ureed al-thahab ela al-matar	أريـد الـذّهاب إلـى المَطـار .
how old are you ?	kam umruk	كَم عُمـرُك ؟
Are you married ?	hal anta motazawij	هَل أنـت مُتَـزوج ؟
I am not married .	ana ghair motazawij	أنـا غـير مُتَـزوج .
Do you have children ?	hal endak abnaa	هَل عِنـدَكَ أبنـاء ؟
No	la	لا
Yes	nam	نَعَـم

Appendix B
Nouns of the Family Member

English Translation	Pronunciation	In Arabic
father	abb	أب
mother	umm	أم
son	iben	إبـن
daughter	bint	بنـت
brother	akh	أخ
sister	ukht	أخـت
wife	zawjeh	زَوجـة
husband	zawj	زَوج
uncle (mother side)	khaal	خال
aunt (mother side)	khalah	خالة
uncle (father side)	amm	عَم
aunt (father side)	ammah	عَمّـة
grandfather	jadd	جَد
grandmother	jaddah	جَـدّة
grandchild	hafeed	حَفيـد
relative (of blood)	qareeb	قريـب
relative (in - law)	naseeb	نسـيب
friend	sahib	صـاحِب
neighbor	jar	جار
cousin (father side .M)	ibin am	إبـن عَم
cousin(mother side .M)	ibin khal	إبـن خال
cousin(father side .F)	bint am	بنـت عَم
cousin (mother side F)	bint khal	بنـت خـال
nephew (brother side)	ibin akh	إبـن أخ
nephew (sister side)	ibin ukht	إبـن أخت
niece (brother side)	bint akh	بنـت اخ
niece (sister side)	bint ukht	بنـت أخت

Appendix C
Parts of the Body

English Translation	Pronunciation	In Arabic
head	rass	راس
hair	sha_er	شَــعِر
ear	uthun	أذن
nose	anf	آنـف
eye	_ayn	عيـن
eyebrows	_hawajib	حَواجـب
eyelashes	rumoosh	رُموش
skin	jild	جِلـد
neck	raqabeh	رَقبـة
hand	yed	يَـد
leg	rejel	رجـل
heart	qalb	قلـب
chest	_seder	صِـدر
abdomen	ba_tin	بَطِـن
stomach	m_edeh	مِعْـده
kidney	kelyeh	كِليـه
liver	kebed	كَبِـد
belly button	_sorrah	صُـرَّه
pelvis	_hoa_d	حوض
bones	_azem	عَظِـم
muscles	_adalat	عَضَــلات
back	_zaher	ظهـر
knee	rokbeh	رُكْبـه
finger	o_sba_q	أصْــبَع
nail	o_zfar	أظْفـر
beauty spot	shameh	شـامِه
blood vessels	_orooq	عُروق

Appendix D
Words of Nature

English Translation	Pronunciation	In Arabic
tree	shajarah	شَــجَرة
road	ṯareeq	طَــريق
farm	mazra-ah	مَزرَعـه
orchard	bustan	بُســتان
forest	ghabeh	غابـة
sky	samaa	سَماء
earth	arḏ	أرض
cloud	ghaim	غيـم
rain	shitaa	شِــتاء
sun	shams	شَــمس
moon	qamar	قَــمَر
sea	baḥar	بَحَــر
ocean	muḥeeṯ	مُحيـط
dessert	saḥraa	صَــحْراء
winds	ri-yaḥ	ريـاح
grass	ḥasheesh	حَشــيش
flowers	ward	وَرَد
bugs	ḥasharat	حَشَــرات
fog	ḏabab	ضَــباب
stars	nujoom	نْجـوم
space	faḏaa	قَضَــاء
thunder	ra-ed	رَعِـد
lightning	barq	بَــرق
hail	barad	بَــرْد

Appendix E
Clothing and Accessories

English Translation	Pronunciation	In Arabic
dress	fustan	فُسْـــــتان
pants	banṭaloon	بَنطَلْـــون
skirt	tannoorah	تَنّـــورة
scarf	mindeel	مِنـــديل
hat	ṭaqeyyah	طاقِيَّـــة
shoes	ḥithaa	حِذاء
shirt	qameeṣ	قمیـــص
jacket	jakait	جاكيـت
suite	badleh	بَدْلِـــه
fabric	qimash	قِمــاش
button	zerr	زر
zipper	saḥhab	سَـــحّاب
thread	khaiṭ	خيـط
earring	ḥalaq	حَلَـــق
bracelet	iswarah	إسوارة
eyeglasses	naẓ-ẓarah	نظّـارة
ring	khatim	خـاتِم
wallet	maḥfaẓah	مَحْفظـه
necklace	ṭaoq	طوق
anklet	khilkhal	خِلْخـــال
jewelry	mojawharat	مُجَوهَـرات
purse	ḥaqeebat yad	حَقيبَـــة يَـد
socks	jarabat	جَرَبـــات

71

Appendix F
Things in The House

English Translation	Pronunciation	In Arabic
chair	kursee	كُرسـي
table	tawlih	طاولـه
bed	takhit	تَخـت
closet	khazanih	خَزانـه
sofa	kanabayih	كَنبايــه
door	bab	بـاب
window	shubbak	شُــبّاك
wall	ha-it	حـائط
bathroom	hammam	حَمَّـام
bedroom	ghurfit nome	غرفـة نـوم
dining room	ghurfit ta-am	غرفـة طعـام
kitchen	matbakh	مَطبَــخ
family room	ghurfit juloos	غرفـة جُلـوس
living room	ghurfit di-yoof	غرفـة ضـيوف
roof	saqif	سَــقف
mattress	farsheh	فَرشـه
comforter	lihaf	لِحـاف
blanket	bataniyyeh	بَطانيــه
pillow	makhaddih	مَخَـدة
bed sheet	sharshaf	شَرشَــف
picture frame	lowhah	لوحـه
clock	sa-ah	ساعه
bulb	lambah	لَمبـه

Appendix G
Things in The Kitchen

English Translation	Pronunciation	in arabic
refrigerator	thallajeh	ثلّاجِـــه
oven	furon	فـــرُن
faucet	hanafeyyeh	حَنَفَّيِـــه
water	maa	ماء
plate	sahin	صَـــحِن
cup	finjan	فِنجــان
tray	seeneyyeh	صـــينيَّه
pitcher	ibreeq	إبـــريق
food	ta-am	طعـام
cooking pot	tanjarah	طنْجَـــره
sugar	sukkar	سـكر
salt	milih	مِلِـــح
bowl	zobdeyyeh	زُبْديَـــه
basket	salleh	سَـــلّة
spoon	mil-aqah	مِلْعَقَـــة
fork	shoakeh	شـــوكة
knife	sikkeen	سِـــكين
sink	majla	مَجْلـــى
spices	biharat	بهـارات
apron	maryool	مَـــرْيُول
towel	bashkeer	بَشْـــكير
glass	zujaj	زُجــاج
dish washer	jallayeh	جَلّايِـــه
vase	mazhareyeh	مَزْهَرِيِـــه
strainer	misfayeh	مِصْـــفايه
soap	saboon	صـابون
sponge	isfinjeh	إسـفِنجه

Appendix H
Common Produce

English Translation	Pronunciation	In Arabic
fruit	fawa-keh	فَواكِـه
orange	burtuqal	بُرثُقَـال
banana	moaz	موز
grapes	enab	عِنـب
pomegranate	rum-man	رُمَـان
watermelon	bat-teekh	بَطّيـخ
cantaloupe	shum-mam	شُـمّام
guava	jaw-wafeh	جَوافـه
apricot	meshmesh	مِشْـمِشْ
peach	dur-raq	دُراق
raspberry	toot	تـوت
apple	tuf-fah	ثُقّـاح
strawberry	farawleh	قراولــه
vegetables	khudra-wat	خُضْـرَوَات
zucchini / squash	koosa	كوسـا
eggplant	beathinjan	بيثِنجـان
cabbage	malfoof	ملفـوف
lettuce	khass	خَـس
lemon	laymoon	ليْمـون
tomato	bandoorah	بَنـدوره
cucumber	khi-yar	خِيـار
carrots	jazar	جَـزَر
parsley	baqdooniss	بَقْـدونيِس
onion	basal	بَصَـل
green pepper	fil-fil akhdar	فِلفِـل أخْضَـر
sweet peas	bazailla	بـازلاً
green beans	fa-soolya	فاصـوليا

74

Appendix I
Colors

English Translation	Pronunciation	In Arabic
blue	azraq	أزْرَق
green	akhdar	أخْضَــر
yellow	asfar	أصْـــفر
red	ahmar	أحمَر
orange	burtuqali	بُرْثُقَـــــالي
violet	banafsajee	بَنَفْسَــــجي
gray	sakanie	سَــكَني
black	aswad	أسْــوَد
white	abyad	أبْيَــــض

Days of the Week

English Translation	Pronunciation	In Arabic
Saturday	Al-sabit	السَـــبت
Sunday	Al-ahad	الأحَـد
Monday	Al-ethnain	الإثنيــــن
Tuesday	Al-thulathaa	الثُلاثــــاء
Wednesday	Al-arbeaa	الأربعــــاء
Thursday	Al-khamees	الخَميــس
Friday	Al-jumaa	الجُمعــة

Appendix J
The Four Seasons

English Translation	Pronunciation	In Arabic
spring	rabee	رَبيــــع
summer	saif	صـــيف
fall	khareef	خَــريف
winter	shitaa	شِــــتاء

Months of the Arabic Year (Solar Months)

English Translation	Pronunciation	In Arabic
January	kanoon Al-thani	كـانون الثــاني
February	shubat	شـــباط
March	athar	آذار
April	nissan	نيســـان
May	ayyar	أيَــــار
June	Huzayran	حُـــزَيران
July	Tammoz	تَمـــوز
August	Abb	آب
September	Aylool	أيلـــول
October	Teshreen Al-awal	تِشــــرين الأول
November	Teshreen Al-thani	تِشـــرين ألثــاني
December	Kanoon Al-awal	كـانون الأول

Appendix K
Months of the Muslim Year (Lunar Months)

Pronunciation	In Arabic
Muharram	مُحَــرَّم
Safar	صَــفر
Rabi Al-awal	رَبيـــع الأوَّل
Rabi Al-thani	رَبيـــع الثّـــاني
Jamadi Al-awal	جَمـادي الأوَّل
Jamadi Al-thani	جَمـادي الثّـــاني
Rajab	رَجَـب
Shaban	شَـــعبان
Ramadan	رَمَضـــان
Shawwal	شَـــوَّال
Thu Al-qidah	ذو القعـــدة
Thu Al-hijah	ذو الحِجـــة

Note: These months follow the lunar months and are composed of 29 or 30 days. Therefore, these months vary from year to year with their solar months equivalence.

Appendix L
Numbers

English Translation	Pronunciation	In Arabic
one	wahid	واحِد
two	ithnan	إثنــان
three	thalathah	ثلاثــة
four	arba-ah	أربَعــة
five	khamsah	خَمسـة
six	sittah	سِـتّة
seven	sab-ah	سَــبْعة
eight	thamaneyah	ثمانيــة
nine	tis-ah	تِسْــعة
ten	asharah	عَشَــرة
eleven	ahada ashur	أحَدَ عَشَــر
twelve	ithna ashur	إثْنــا عَشَــر
thirteen	thalathata ashur	ثلاثــة عَشَــر
fourteen	arbata ashur	أربَعــة عَشَــر
fifteen	khamsata ashur	خَمسَــة عَشَــر
sixteen	sittata ashur	سِــتّة عَشَــر
seventeen	sab-ata ashur	سَــبعَة عَشَــر
eighteen	thamaniyata ashur	ثمانيَــة عَشَــر
nineteen	tes-ata ashur	تِسْــعَة عَشَــر
twenty	eshroon	عِشْــرون

Directions

English Translation	Pronunciation	In Arabic
north	shamal	شَــمال
south	janoob	جَنــوب
east	sharq	شَــرق
west	gharb	غَــرب

Appendix M
Counting in Tens

English Translation	Pronunciation	In Arabic
ten	asharah	عَشَـرة
twenty	eshroon	عِشْـرون
thirty	thalathoon	ثلاثُـون
forty	arba-oon	أربَعُـون
fifty	khamsoon	خَمْسُـون
sixty	settoon	سِـتّون
seventy	sab-oon	سَـبْعون
eighty	thamanoon	ثمَـانون
ninety	tes-oon	تِسْـعون
hundred	ma-ah	مائـه

Counting in Hundreds

English Translation	pronunciation	In Arabic
one hundred	ma-ah	مائـه
two hundred	ma-atan	مائتـان
three hundred	thalath mi-ah	ثـلاث مِنـة
four hundred	arba mi-ah	أربَـع مِنـة
five hundred	khams mi-ah	خَمس مِنـة
six hundred	set mi-ah	سِـت مِنـة
seven hundred	sabe mi-ah	سَـبع مِنـة
eight hundred	thamani mi-ah	ثمـاني مِنـة
nine hundred	tes-a mi-ah	تِسْـع مِنـة
one thousand	alf	ألـف

Appendix N
Things in the street

English Translation	Pronunciation	In Arabic
car	sayyarah	سَــيّارة
truck	sha<u>h</u>inah	شـــاحِنه
bus	ba<u>s</u>	بــاص
motorcycle	darrajah nareyyah	دَرّاجـه ناريّـه
bike	darrajah hawa-eyyeh	دَرّاجـه هَوائيّـــه
street	shar<u>i</u>	شــارع
sidewalk	ra<u>s</u>eef	رَصـــيف
way	<u>t</u>areeq	طـــريق
traffic light	isharah <u>d</u>ow-eyyah	إشـارة ضَـــــونيه
alley	dakhleh	دَخلـه
up hill	<u>t</u>al<u>a</u>h	طَلعـه
down hill	nazleh	نزلـه
parking	mowkif	مَوْقِــف
market place	sowq	ســوق
store	dukkan	دُكّــان
gas station	kaziyyeh	كازيـــه
pole	<u>a</u>mood	عامـود
tree	shajarah	شَــجَره
stop sign	isharet woqoof	إشـارة وُقـوف
detour	ta<u>h</u>weeleh	تَحويلــه
no entry	mamno<u>o</u> al-moroor	مَمنـوع المرور
yield	entabeh	إنتَبـــه
house	bayt	بَيْـت

Appendix O
Animal Names

English Translation	Pronunciation	In Arabic
dog	kalb	كلــب
cat	hirrah	هِرّة
turtle	sulhufah	ســـلحُفاة
horse	hisan	حِصــان
donkey	himar	حِمـار
cow	baqarah	بَقــــرة
calf	ejel	عِجِــل
goat	anzah	عَنـزه
sheep	kharoof	خاروف
chicken	dajajah	دَجاجـة
roaster	deek	ديـك
fox	thalub	ثعّلــــب
wolf	thieb	ذِنـــب
bird	tair	طـيـر
mouse	farah	فــارة
rat	jardoon	جَـردون
frog	difda	ضِــفَدَع
turkey	habash	حَبَــش
duck	but	بَـط
camel	jamal	جَمَـل
bull	thowr	ثـور
lizard	hardoon	حَـردون
owl	boomeh	بومـة
craw	ghurab	غُراب

Appendix P
Professions / jobs

English Translation	Pronunciation	In Arabic
doctor	ṭabeeb	طَبِيـب
nurse	mumarriḏ	مُمَـرِّض
teacher	mudarris	مُـدَرِّس
engineer	muhandis	مُهَنّـدِس
actor	mumathil	مُمَثِّـل
broadcaster	muthee	مُـذيع
writer	katib	كاتِـب
artist	ras-sam	رسـام
president	ra-ees	رَئِيـس
king	malik	مَلِـك
governor	muḥafiẓ	مُحـافِظ
minister	wazeer	وَزيـر
butcher	laḥ-ham	لحـام
carpenter	naj-jar	نجـار
barber	ḥal-laq	حَـلّاق
servant	khadem	خـادِم
cook	ṭab-bakh	طَبّـاخ
nanny	murabbi-yeh	مُرَبّيـه
driver	sa-iq	ســائق
sewer	khay-yaṭ	خَيّـاط
principal	mudeer	مُـدير
scientist	ᵃlim	عـالم
banker	maṣrifiy	مَصـرفي
worker	ᵃmil	عامل
bread maker	khab-baz	خَبّـاز
drycleaner	kaw-wa	كـوّى